Russian Tortoises

Complete Herp Care

E. J. Pirog

Russian Tortioses

Project Team
Editor: Thomas Mazorlig
Assistant Editor: Brian M. Scott
Copy Editor: Carl Schutt
Cover Design: Cándida Moreira Tómassini
Design Team: Mary Ann Kahn & Patty Escabi

T.F.H. Publications
President/CEO: Glen S. Axelrod
Executive Vice President: Mark E. Johnson
Publisher: Christopher T. Reggio
Production Manager: Kathy Bontz

T.F.H. Publications, Inc.
One TFH Plaza
Third and Union Avenues
Neptune City, NJ 07753

05 06 07 08 09   1 3 5 7 9 8 6 4 2

Library of Congress Cataloging-in-Publication Data
Pirog, Edward.-Russian tortoises : a complete guide to testudo / Edward Pirog.
p. cm.
Includes bibliographical references and index.
ISBN 0-7938-2882-1 (alk. paper)
1. Central Asian tortoises as pets. I. Title.
SF459.T8P57 2005
639.3'924--dc22
2005017800

The Leader In Responsible Animal Care For Over 50 Years!™
www.tfhpublications.com

Table of Contents

Tortoises have been kept as pets for hundreds of years. The attractive appeal of these charming creatures is one that is difficult to resist. That appeal probably stems from the impression that a pet tortoise rarely shows aggression, fear, anger, or any of the other negative traits that we experience in our daily lives. Tortoises appear to be one the most peaceful creatures that walk the earth, seemingly without a care in the world. It is relaxing to watch a tortoise go about its daily routine.

Of all the tortoises that have been kept as pets in the past and present, the tortoises of the Mediterranean region may be the most popular. The Mediterranean tortoises are quite a common sight throughout many of the gardens of Europe. The practice of keeping tortoises as pets seems to equally have spread throughout the United States. It is the intent of this guide to provide an introduction to the care and maintenance of the Mediterranean tortoises with particular focus on the Russian tortoise, *Testudo horsfieldi*. While as much information as possible will be provided, the primary purpose of this guide is to provide a good foundation for and a basic understanding of caring for these tortoises as pets.

Introduction

It should be noted here that there are many tortoise books on the market today, and it would seem that there is a great contradiction in styles, information, and methods that are presented. What needs to be understood from the start is that there is no one single way to maintain these wonderful creatures in captivity. Because they are cold-blooded and are usually kept as pets well outside of their natural range, it quickly comes to light that there are many variables that are dependent on one another. Changing one or more of those variables can usually be compensated for or can lead to a change in another. It is for this reason that it is highly recommended that as much information as possible be gathered in the quest to properly care for the pet tortoise and to provide the most acceptable conditions for a particular pet tortoise. Along with the gathered information, it is also important to pay particular attention to the pet tortoise and see how it responds to the particular keeping conditions put in place by the keeper. It is the tortoise itself that is the best telltale indicator as to whether the conditions provided are acceptable to it or not. A Russian tortoise and its cousins, if properly cared for, can provide you with many years of enjoyment. It is my hope that with the aid of this guide, your experience will be an easy and pleasant one.

Chapter 1

Species Accounts and Natural History

While you may think of your tortoise as a pet, it is essentially a wild animal. Even if you buy a captive-bred (more on that term later) baby, it is still only one or two generations removed from the wild. To better understand your tortoise and its needs, you will need to understand something of its habitat and behavior in the wild.

Taxonomy

To understand the types of tortoises covered in this volume, you need to have a little understanding of the biological field of taxonomy. Taxonomy is simply the study of the naming of biological organisms. The purpose of this is to standardize the names of organisms with the

Turtle Terms

Here are some terms that will help you find your way around your tortoise.

Carapace: the top part of the shell

Plastron: the bottom part of the shell

Scutes: the individual plates that make up the shell

Marginals: the scutes on the outer edge of the carapace

Supracaudal: the scute directly above the tail

Nuchal: the scute directly above the neck

External anatomy of *Testudo* using a Hermann's tortoise as an example.

Scutes

Carapace

Nuchal

Supracaudal

Marginals

Plastron

hope of making communication between biologists easier and less confusing. At the time taxonomic structure was created, the language of choice was Latin, the accepted language of most of the scientific community.

Taxonomy originally classified organisms based on specific anatomical structures, but the recent trend is to group organisms together that appear to be related to each other. To do this, the forms, structure, habits, habitat, and genetics of organisms are compared. Similar organisms are grouped together.

The taxonomic system is called a *binomial system* because each organism has a two part name. The first name is the genus (plural: genera) and the second is the species. The genus is capitalized and the species is lower case, and both names are set in italics; so the Russian tortoise is known in scientific circles as *Testudo horsfieldii*. A number of similar species form the genus. The next step above the genus is the family, and it is composed of a group of related genera. When populations or groups within a species show some differences but not enough differences to be considered separate species, they are often considered subspecies.

Today, the taxonomy of tortoises in general is controversial. This guide is going to follow the taxonomy that is widely accepted, and subspecies will be mentioned but will not be specifically covered to keep the information simple. If you would like to delve into the topic in more detail, consult the list of references at the end of this guide to find sources that might help you in understanding the situation better. For the sake of simplicity, the taxonomy that is going to be followed here can be found in the box to the right.

This guide is going to describe the different species that are covered here in a geographical context, starting with the species that ranges the furthest north.

Testudo Taxonomy

Kingdom: Animalia

Phyllum: Chodata

Class: Reptilia

Order: Testudines, the turtles

Family: Testudinidae, the tortoises

Genus: *Testudo*, the Mediterranean tortoises

Species: *Testudo graeca*, Greek Tortoise

T. hermanni, Hermann's Tortoise

T. horsfieldii, Russian Tortoise

T. kleinmanni, Egyptian Tortoise

T. marginata, Marginated Tortoise

Russian Tortoise, *Testudo horsfieldii*

The Russian tortoise has the northernmost range of all the *Testudo*. Its range extends from the area of the Caspian Sea east through Kazakhstan to western Xinjiang, China and south to Iran, Afghanistan, and Pakistan. This tortoise has long been known as *Testudo horsfieldii*, but because of accepted differences from other *Testudo*, it is becoming widely accepted as *Agrionemys horsfieldii*.

Description

The distinguishing character traits for *T. horsfieldii* are that it is as long as it is wide, the overall profile is relatively flattened when compared to the other *Testudo*, the plastron is not hinged between the hindmost scutes and the next row of scutes forward of that, and it has four claws on each foot. The Russian tortoise's general appearance is usually a straw-yellow color with black markings in the middle of each scute, but they can be of a uniform dark olive green to black color or missing dark markings entirely. They can reach a size of 9 to 10 inches (22.8 to 25.4 cm) long with males being somewhat smaller than females.

Typical example of a Russian tortoise. This species is the most round-looking of the *Testudo*.

Habitat

The habitat that the Russian tortoise occupies is a very harsh one. It is typified by dry, sandy soil and sparsely covered by short grasses and shrubs. This seems to be the preferred habitat, although the Russian tortoise has been found everywhere from rocky slopes to low-lying drainage areas to cultivated areas. It is not often found in forested areas.

It makes its home in rodent burrows and rock crevices in addition to digging its own burrows in well-drained areas. During the times of harsh weather—either too cold or too hot—it will burrow down into the earth or go deep into burrows to escape the life-threatening climatic conditions. The Russian tortoise is most active when the temperature ranges from 68° to 90°F (20° to 32.2°C). In the higher mountain areas and the northern limits of its range, the tortoise is active from late spring to early fall. During this time, it is most active in the early morning with a secondary activity period in the late afternoon.

When the temperatures climb above the preferred range, the activity pattern will shift to earlier hours in the morning and to later hours in the evening. In the southern part of its range, it can extend its total season of activity, but it must seek shelter during the hottest part of the summer. At this time, it will estivate (go dormant to escape the heat) until the average temperatures drop to a suitable level.

The Round Tortoise

To the untrained eye, it can be difficult to tell Russian tortoises from their other relatives. To add to the difficulty, some pet suppliers will house Russian tortoises and Greek tortoises together and may not themselves distinguish between the two. One easy way to separate Russian tortoises from the others is to look at them from above. Russian tortoises are circular in shape, while the other species are oval or rectangular. Another difference is that the Russians are relatively flat, and the other species have more of a dome.

During the cold winter months, it will hibernate to survive the unfavorable conditions. Studies have shown that during the cold weather temperatures the Russian tortoise tends to seek out areas where the temperature ranges from 43° to 50°F (6.1° to 10°C). The Russian tortoise will come out of its hibernation or estivation if temperatures fall into favorable ranges, and this can be risky for the animal. If the tortoise is caught out in the open when the temperatures return to normal for that particular period, it could succumb to the extreme high or low temperatures.

Diet

The Russian tortoise is an opportunistic feeder (as are most tortoises). It feeds on a wide range of plants, limited only by its ability to reach them. This tortoise is not normally in the habit of grazing on grasses but focuses on broad leafy plants. The tortoise will continue to feed on the dried plants long after the plant has died in the winter or during dry spells. The Russian tortoise also feeds on the leaves, flowers, fruits, and berries that fall off of trees and bushes. The tortoise will consume insects and animal feces in addition to plant material. During periods when the tortoise is still active but food is scarce, it will to travel great distances in its search for food. While the Russian tortoise can go through long periods without water, it does drink large amounts when available.

Russian tortoises are opportunistic herbivores, browsing on whatever plants are available in their harsh habitat.

Estivation vs. Hibernation

These two terms are used to describe the process of going into a state of dormancy during a period of harsh weather conditions and/or food scarcity. While the two terms are similar, they are not exactly the same. The term hibernation is used to describe a period of dormancy in the winter, used by animals to escape the cold and avoid starvation. Estivation describes a dormancy period during the summer or dry season, used by animals to avoid dehydration, overheating, and starvation. Most *Testudo* both hibernate and estivate.

Breeding

Breeding season begins with emergence of the tortoise from hibernation. After breeding, it will feed extensively on the new spring growth. The breeding season will vary but, in most cases, will follow the pattern of breeding in early spring with egg deposition in late spring to early summer. Up to 20 eggs can be deposited, but a dozen is the more usual number. These eggs are not deposited all at one time but are spread out over two or three clutches.

The nest site chosen is usually in a shady area out of direct sunlight. The eggs measure in size from 1.25 to 2.25 inches long (3.2 to 5.7 cm) and will hatch in 40 to 60 days. The eggs hatch in late summer to early fall, and the hatchlings remain in the nest until the following year. The hatchlings survive on the yolk reserves that are absorbed from the egg. On emergence from the nest, the hatchlings face a multitude of dangers, including predation from many animals such as foxes, crows, and monitor lizards. The hatchlings also run a high risk of dying from the elements and general exposure.

If the tortoise is lucky or strong enough, it can reach breeding size in approximately 10 years or so. Breeding size for adults is 4 to 5 inches (10.2 to 12.7 cm) for the males and 5 to 6 inches (12.7 to 15.2 cm) for the females. The time it takes to reach maturity varies greatly throughout the Russian tortoise's natural range and depends on average temperature and food availability. The male Russian tortoise often has a large home range, while the female is more localized. This is noticeable during the breeding season and is subject to change as the year progresses and food availability becomes more sparse.

Greek Tortoise, *Testudo graeca*

The Greek Tortoise has a range that extends from southwestern Europe and Yugoslavia to Iran and Turkmenistan to North Africa. In addition, the species has been successfully introduced onto the Canary Islands, Sardinia, and Sicily and to France and Italy.

Description

The distinguishing character trait for *Testudo graeca* is the presence of a conical scale on the back side of the thigh. (This particular trait has given rise to the other common name for this tortoise, the spur-thighed tortoise.) There is also no horny scale present on the tip of the tail. The plastron is hinged at the forward opening of the rear legs.

There are several recognized forms of *Testudo graeca*, and there is a great deal of debate on the exact number of subspecies that should be recognized. The most important point to remember—from the standpoint of a tortoise keeper—is that because of the extent of the range of the Greek tortoise, there are populations that are not inclined to hibernate. Those that come from North Africa and the

Greek Tortoises Aren't Greek

One interesting note in the nomenclature for *Testudo graeca* is that the common name used for the Greek tortoise does not come from the tortoise living in Greece—although it does. It comes from the belief that the markings on its shell appear similar to Greek mosaic tiles.

The Greek tortoise varies considerably across its range. This individual is from Morocco.

Middle East do not experience temperatures cold enough to induce true hibernation. The European forms of Greek tortoise that occur in the northern part of the range do experience such temperatures and are inclined to hibernate during the winter. Those tortoises in the southern part of this range estivate when the temperatures rise above a tolerable level. The forms of *T. graeca* that usually experience estivation are those that originate in North Africa.

Habitat

The habitat the Greek tortoise prefers is much like that of the Russian tortoise. It occurs in areas of grassy flatlands with low-lying shrubbery to open grassland. It avoids areas of steep rocky slopes, although it is found in the transition zone of such areas. It prefers dry, well-drained, sandy areas and is not commonly found in moist areas. The Greek tortoise also seems to tolerate cultivated areas better than any of the other *Testudo*. In many countries, the Greek tortoise is seen as a competitor for grazing animals and, as such, is sometime destroyed to eliminate that competition.

In the northern part of its range, the Greek tortoise becomes active in early spring, and breeding usually takes place during March to April. On emergence from hibernation, the male will aggressively seek a female and can mate multiple times on a given day. The male can become extremely aggressive at this time and may even inflict injury on the female. Male-to-male interaction is usually limited to the breeding season and consists of competition for a female. Two or more males mating alternately with a single female has been observed over a given mating season.

In the southern portion of the range, the breeding cycles seem to occur with the same cues as the northern race except that the tortoises don't actually hibernate. The winter season is usually marked by a cool rainy period with spring bringing an emergence of plant growth. This seems to be the cue for breeding in the southernmost range of *T. graeca*. Although the southern forms do not actually hibernate, they do have a winter rest or slowdown period when there is a decrease in activity.

These Greek tortoises are from Libyan stock.

Diet

The Greek tortoise diet consists of broadleaf weeds, which have a seasonal lifecycle, in addition to grasses. The tortoise seems to focus on the top of the various food plants, consuming the flowers, seeds, berries, and new growth. Insects and other animal matter are occasionally consumed, but this makes up a small portion of the diet. Overall, the Greek tortoise has a diet preference that is very similar to the Russian tortoise's but with a higher preference for grasses.

Breeeding

Breeding takes place on emergence from hibernation with nesting occurring in late spring to early summer. The nesting site chosen for the northern forms is usually located in an area that receives direct sunlight. In contrast, the southern forms will nest in an area that is protected from direct sunlight. How the female actually selects the site is not fully known, but the female is very careful as to how she selects the site. The female will smell the ground and explore many areas. When a site is selected she will scratch the ground with her forelimbs and turn around and continue digging with the hind limbs. If the ground is very dry, she will urinate to soften up the ground and continue digging.

Up to seven eggs can be deposited, but two to four is the more usual clutch size. The eggs measure 30 to 40 mm long and can take up to four months to hatch, but 60 to 90 days is the more typical time for hatching. One female can nest up to four times in a year, but the typical pattern is to have two nestings per year. At least 30 days pass between each nesting. Nesting usually takes place in the early morning hours or the late afternoon. Depending on the temperature, the tortoise can take up to two hours to complete the entire process. On completion of the nest, the female will pack the surface of the nest down and cover it with the surrounding ground litter. She will then move to another area way from the nest site and disturb it. This behavior probably throws off nest predators.

Female Greek tortoises can take up to twelve years to reach maturity, and the males may take as long as seven years. The actual adult size varies depending on the race. Both the northern and southern forms will reach maturity at a size of 8 to 10 inches (20.3 to 25.4 cm), but there are some smaller races that will mature at 6 to 8 inches (15.2 to 20.3 cm). The smaller races usually originate from the harshest and most desert-like environments within the natural range.

Hermann's Tortoise, *Testudo hermanni*

The Hermann's tortoise occurs on the Islas Baleares of Spain and from southern France eastward to European Turkey and Rumania. It is also found on Sardinia and Corsica.

Description

The distinguishing characteristics for the Hermann's tortoise are a supracaudal scale that is usually undivided, a horn-shaped scale at the tip of the tail, and no hinge on the plastron forward of the opening for rear legs. There are two forms of Hermann's tortoises commonly found in the pet trade with the size of the adults being the most distinguishing factors. The western form is smaller, more highly domed, and usually has more distinguishing markings than the eastern form, which is larger and flatter.

Habitat

The habitat that the Hermann's tortoise occupies is similar to other *Testudo* in that it is warm. However, the Hermann's tortoise preference differs in that it seems to favor a more moist or humid environment, such as that found in meadows and forest edges. They have also adapted fairly well to cultivated areas.

Diet

The Hermann's tortoise diet differs from most of the other *Testudo* in that this species consumes

Hermann's tortoise occurs in two recognized subspecies, *T. hermanni hermanni* (the two small individuals) and *T. hermanni robertmertensi* (the large individual).

more insects and animal matter, although plant material is still the majority of the diet. Plants that are normally consumed include leguminous plants in addition to seasonal leafy greens, fruits, and berries.

Breeding

Breeding occurs on roughly the same schedule as the other *Testudo*. Breeding commences in the spring upon emergence from hibernation. Nesting takes place in late spring to early summer. Nests are usually constructed in areas of partial sunlight. The female will deposit up to twelve eggs, but four to six is the more typical clutch size. One to three clutches of eggs can be deposited per year, with one or two clutches being average. The period between clutches is usually 40 days or more. Hatchlings emerge in 60 to 90 days.

Sexual maturity is reached in six to eight years for the males and 10 to 12 years for the females. The size of the mature female is 7 to 8 inches (17.8 to 20.3 cm) for the western race and 7 to 9 inches (17.8 to 22.9 cm) for the eastern race.

Marginated Tortoise, *Testudo marginata*

The marginated tortoise ranges over Greece and extreme southern Albania. It has also been successfully introduced on Sardinia and in Tuscany, Italy.

Description

Specific character traits for *Testudo marginata* include an elongated carapace, four to five longitudinal rows of enlarged scales on the forelimbs, and supracaudal and posterior marginals that are greatly flared outward. It is from this trait that the marginated tortoise gets its name.

Habitat

Information on the natural history of the marginated tortoise is not well documented, mainly because of its habitat preference and fairly restricted range. What is known is that it has much the same habitat preference as the Hermann's tortoise, with the exception that it favors areas of thick and virtually impenetrable underbrush. It can also be found in more mountainous terrain. This type of habitat makes observation of the species in the wild difficult.

Diet

The diet of the marginated tortoise is much like the Hermann's in that there is a preference for animal material, such as insects and the like. The main portion of the diet is still seasonal broadleaf greens, berries, and fruit, as in most tortoises.

Breeding

Breeding occurs in the spring with the female nesting in the late spring to early summer. She deposits two to twelve eggs per clutch, and they hatch in 60 to 90 days. One remarkable note to the breeding habits of *T. marginata* is that the male can become extremely viscous toward the female during breeding. The male is so aggressive and massive that the female frequently sustains severe damage, which occasionally leads to her death.

Marginated tortoises are both poorly known in the wild and infrequently kept as pets.

Egyptian Tortoise, *Testudo kleinmanni*

The Egyptian tortoise has the most restricted range of all the *Testudo*. Its range is limited to the coastal margins of north Africa and extreme western Asia, extending from Libya to southern Israel.

Description

The Egyptian tortoise is distinguished from the other *Testudo* by its short carapace, posterior marginal scutes not flared, and three longitudinal rows of enlarged scales on the anterior surface of the forelimbs. *Testudo kleinmanni* also has the smallest adult form of the *Testudo* group, rarely reaching more than 5 inches (12.7 cm) in length.

Occupying a restricted range, the Egyptian tortoise is vulnerable to over-collection and habitat destruction.

Habitat

The preferred habitat of the Egyptian tortoise is coastal sand dunes, dried river beds, and the flood plains of those rivers in its range. The soil is well drained and sparsely vegetated. While it prefers a desert habitat, the tortoise is usually found in association with whatever moisture is available. It does not burrow but will occupy mammal burrows in addition to rock crevices and scrapes in areas protected from the sun.

Diet

Diet for the Egyptian tortoise is very similar to other *Testudo*. Annual broadleaf greens make up the majority of its diet. It is not a grazer for the most part but does consume the new grass that appears with the seasonal rains. The Egyptian tortoise is also an opportunistic feeder that will feed on the carrion and feces of other animals. These items make up a small portion of the diet.

Breeding

Mature males are 3 to 4 inches (7.6 to 10.2 cm) long and the females are 4 to 5 inches (10.2 to 12.7 cm) in length. Breeding takes place in the spring with eggs being deposited in the late spring to early summer. The female can lay up to four eggs but the more common clutch size is one to two eggs. This can be repeated four to five times in a given year with the time between each clutch being approximately 30 to 40 days. More commonly, the female will only have one or two clutches a year. The eggs are elongated measuring 3/4 inch by 1/2 inch (1.9 by 1.3 cm) on the average. The eggs hatch in 70 to 100 days. It is estimated that it takes seven to ten years for the Egyptian tortoise to mature to breeding size.

Predators and Parasites

Similar predators are found throughout the range of all the species of *Testudo*. These predators don't really distinguish one small and tasty tortoise from another. So—with a few exceptions—the predators of one species also prey on the others.

Some of the natural enemies of the Russian tortoise include, foxes, crows, and monitor lizards. These predators also take the other species. Predators are usually not a major threat to the marginated tortoise because of its size, but hatchlings do experience the same predation from the same predators as the other members of the group.

As you may imagine, the size of the Egyptian tortoise gives it a multitude of enemies. The hatchlings are bite-sized for almost any animal and have a high risk of being consumed. It is well

Species Characteristics of *Testudo*

Species	T. graeca	T. hermanni	T. marginata	T. horsfieldi	T. kleinmanni
Max. adult size (in.)	11-12	8-9	12	9-10	5.5
Thigh spurs	yes	no	no	yes	no
Tail scale	no	yes	no	yes	no
Hinged plastron	females only	no	no	no	yes
Front claws	5	5	5	4	5
Supracaudal scutes	1	2	1	1	1
Nuchal scute	narrow	narrow	narrow	small	wide

table adapted from Pursall, 1994.

Endangered Egyptians

Because of their small size and limited range, the Egyptian tortoise is probably the most vulnerable *Testudo* species in nature. It was first officially addressed in the International Union for Conservation of Nature and Natural Resources (IUCN) Red Data Book in 1982, where its status was listed as venerable. Recent studies suggest that its endangered and as a result it has now been listed as an Appendix I animal under the Convention of International Trade of Endangered Species (CITES). This means that the trade of Egyptian tortoises is prohibited. It's suspected that the commercial trade of Egyptian tortoises and the destruction of their natural habitat are the two major causes of the depletion of wild stocks. Therefore, it's highly recommended that only captive born animals be considered as pets.

known that the greatest threat to both the adults and the hatchlings is from the crow, although predation of the Egyptian tortoise is not limited to that animal.

The parasites found throughout the *Testudo* group seem to follow the same pattern as the predators in that they don't seem to distinguish between the different forms of *Testudo*. The most common parasites encountered are ticks, nematodes, and protozoa. Ticks are exceptionally common on Greek tortoises. Because of the harsh environment the Egyptian tortoise comes from, the most common parasites associated with this species are nematodes and protozoa. Ticks are not as commonly found on the Egyptian tortoise as they are with other *Testudo* probably because the environment is so dry.

Summing Up

All of the *Testudo* have similar habits, preferences, and physical appearance, which is why they are grouped in one genus (two genera if you recognize *Agrionemys*). The main differences that do occur are adaptations to the environments in which each can be found. Food preferences, breeding habits, and other life characteristics are usually similar. This should be remembered, because it provides a basic starting point in the care and the upkeep of any of the tortoises mentioned here. What needs to be remembered is that the conditions the tortoise prefers are the ones it has adapted to thrive in, and the tortoise has further adapted responses to the problems encountered in the wild. Sometimes these adaptations serve as cues for another behavioral pattern that is not necessary for survival for the animal in captivity. One example of this is that hibernation is a cue for breeding, which is not a necessity for the survival of the individual.

Chapter 2

Obtaining A New Tortoise

Once you have decided that a pet tortoise would be a pleasant addition to the household, there are many aspects of the keeping tortoises that you must address. The first is to research and plan for the new addition. The better the research and the better the planning, the easier and less stressful the process of adding such a pet to the household will be. It is so much easier and safer for the well-being of the tortoise and the tortoise keeper to have the necessities ready before you bring the tortoise home than to find out after the fact that you are missing some vital component, possibly threatening the very survival of the new pet tortoise.

Before You Buy a Tortoise

When you obtain any pet, you should think seriously about the commitment to giving that pet proper care for the entirety of it's life. When that pet is a tortoise, that commitment could last 40 years or more. Think carefully about your ability to provide such long-term care before you buy one. While no one can be sure how their life is going to change over the course of 40 years, you should commit to caring for the animal for that time or— should circumstances make you unable to provide care— to finding another suitable caregiver to continue that commitment.

Preparations

The important points to take into account before obtaining a tortoise are housing, environmental needs, feeding, and veterinary care, which includes getting the name and location of a specialty veterinarian that has experience with tortoises. When these essential items are considered beforehand, frantically scrambling to fill in the missing pieces can be avoided.

Enclosure and Environment

You must decide whether the tortoise is going to be housed outdoors or indoors and how much space can be allocated to the tortoise. A secure enclosure is important in both the indoor and outdoor situations. For the indoor tortoise, safety from pets and unsupervised children needs to be taken into account. For the outdoor pet, the same items should be considered in addition to protection from the elements and other animals. Along with the size and location of the enclosure, you must also think about the interior furnishings.

With a plan for the enclosure in place, you must consider the environmental needs of your pet. Tortoises, like other reptiles, are poikilotherms, or cold-blooded animals. This does not mean that the animal's blood is cold but refers to the fact that, for the most part, the tortoise is dependent on its environment to provide the body heat that enables the metabolism to function properly. Supplemental heating is normally used in captivity to help maintain a good body temperature. In line with temperature is the need for hydration or humidity. Chapter 3 will provide you with the details on setting up the cage and maintaining the proper environment.

Feeding

Once the enclosure is set up, the next step is to learn what foods the tortoise will need and what kind of feeding schedule should be provided. In the current age of keeping pet tortoises,

there are many options for feeding. An all-plant diet can be provided; an all-manufactured diet is also available in many cases, or a combination of the two can be used. The important point is to find out what items are needed and where they can be found, again, preferably before the tortoise is obtained. Chapter 4 contains complete information on diet and feeding.

Whether you plan to house your tortoise indoors or outdoors, have the enclosure completely set up before you bring it home.

Medical Care

The next major consideration is to make sure you have a plan to follow in the event the tortoise gets sick or is injured. The minimum requirement for this plan is to get a list of veterinarians that are in the area and try to find some who specialize in the care and treatment of tortoises. The veterinarians who fall under this classification are considered exotic pet veterinarians and are usually listed as such. It is a good idea to have the name or names of veterinarians before one is actually needed because it makes an emergency less critical and easier to deal with. Chapter 6 covers health care and veterinary issues.

From all that has been written so far in this section, it should be clear that a tortoise is not for everyone. One actually requires a little more care in many cases than a pet dog or cat, but the work of providing that care can be minimized with some good planning. These thoughts were given to present an idea of what to expect before bringing home a tortoise. With all this in mind, the task of acquiring the new tortoise is the next step.

Be Prepared to Hibernate

There is one special issue that a new owner of a Russian tortoise (or other Mediterranean tortoise) needs to be concerned with, and that is the issue of hibernation. If the captive environmental conditions are allowed to get too cool, they will be inclined to hibernate, and if the conditions are allowed to get too hot they will be inclined to estivate. In both cases, the tortoise slows down in order to conserve energy and goes into a kind of sleep mode. Hibernation and estivation are important concepts for the new owner to understand. Information on hibernation and estivation is in Chapter 5.

Obtaining a Russian Tortoise
Pet Shops

The local pet shop is usually the first place most people consider when they want to acquire a tortoise. There are many types of pet shops and each has its advantages as well as disadvantages. The variety of shops can extend from the small local pet shop to the national chain stores.

To begin with, the local, privately owned pet shop can be a good place to obtain a tortoise because the shop owner has a vested interest in the sale. This works to the benefit of the new tortoise owner because the owner of the shop wants to encourage the keeper to continue coming back for food and other necessities. Often, there is a high level of personal attention given to the customer. If there are any problems, the private shop owner is usually willing to work a little harder in order to resolve those problems. The major disadvantage of purchasing a tortoise from the small shop is that most shops concentrate on the more common pets like dogs, cats, and birds, and the staff may have only a limited knowledge of how to keep tortoises. There are exceptions, of course. In small shops, it is not uncommon to see several different tortoises housed together, which is not a good practice.

A subtype of the privately owned pet store is the specialty reptile shop. This kind of pet shop deals with exotic pets and, in many cases, almost exclusively with reptiles and amphibians. It is this kind of specialty shop that is most likely the best resource for obtaining a new tortoise. It has many of the advantages of a small shop added to the benefit of a good knowledge base. Many of the shopkeepers who own or operate such pet shops started out as reptile enthusiasts themselves, so they are well in tune with the needs of their customers. It is in the specialty shop that you can be relatively certain that the tortoise you are getting is healthy and well cared for. Because these shops usually have a knowledgeable staff, it is not very likely you will come across substandard animals or unacceptable husbandry practices. There is one disadvantage here and it is that these shops are not very common and are usually only found around the bigger cities.

The last major type of pet shop is the big chain or department store-type pet shop. It is in this kind of shop you will usually find good deals as far as price and convenience go. The salespeople who usually work in the chain store, even though well intentioned, are usually lacking in a knowledge of tortoise keeping, in addition to being responsible for many different types of animals. Many of the larger chain stores have tried to address this by providing training classes for the workers that take care of the different departments, including the reptile department.

Here are some added tips to keep in mind if considering a pet shop when trying to decide where to purchase your Russian tortoise. A good indication of the quality of the store you are dealing with is the first impression. It is a good idea to take notice of the animal enclosures to be sure they are generally clean. Pay particular attention to see that the water bowls are filled with clean water. Look to see that the enclosures are relatively spacious and the animals are not crowded or contain more than one type of tortoise. A shop that presents itself well, is well organized, and gives the appearance of being well maintained is providing a good indication that it places high importance on the animals and their care.

Many pet sellers house the different species of Testudo together, a practice that facilitates the spread of disease.

HERMAN'S TORTOISE
-Testudo hermani

HORSFIELD'S TORTOISE   pair MAL
aka: Russian Tort
-Testudo horsfiel

In addition to pet shops, there are a number of other outlets where you can obtain a Russian tortoise. Here are some descriptions to give you some idea of what you will be looking for when investigating some of these outlets.

Reptile Shows

The reptile show (also called herp shows, reptile expos, and similar terms) is a swap meet where amphibians, reptiles, and supplies are sold and traded by all forms of reptile-related businesses and private hobbyists. These swap meets can be as small as 15 tables at a high school gym in a small community to as large as hundreds of tables at a large convention center in a major city. At many of the larger shows people come from all over the world to both buy and sell amphibians and reptiles. This can be quite a sight to see for the person who is just beginning to get involved in the keeping of tortoises. At the smaller shows, there are fewer vendors resulting in less selection, but it is much easier to get information on a personal level from the seller than at large, crowded shows.

If you can find the tortoise you are looking for at a show, it is here that you will also usually get your best deal in both price and quality of tortoise. Unfortunately, it is also at the reptile shows that your risk for being taken advantage of can also increase. Therefore, it is always a good idea to go with someone who is familiar with the environment. Many of the vendors are private individuals who attend the shows sporadically. If you do purchase your tortoise from such a person, be sure to

Turtle & Tortoise Societies

Many areas of the United States (and some other countries) have a local turtle and tortoise society. To find out if there is one in your area, check at the local pet shop, on a local library bulletin board, or on the Internet. The members of local turtle and tortoise clubs are usually more than happy and willing to provide help and guidance to the budding tortoise keeper. The society members should be able to direct you to reputable sources of tortoises, supplies, and veterinary care. Some societies have regular meetings with guest speakers, slide shows, and other interesting activities. There are also herpetological societies, which perform the same activities but are more broadly focused to include those interested in all types of reptiles and amphibians. Both types of societies normally have a membership fee, but it is usually affordable.

All the species of *Testudo* are being bred in captivity to some extent. These are baby *T. graeca*.

get as much information as you can. Not only should you get as much information about the tortoise in terms of its care and history, but also get as much contact information about the vendor as possible. If anything does go wrong or you have any more questions about your new tortoise, you will have someone to turn to.

Breeders

Many of the vendors who participate in the reptile shows are breeders of the species they are selling. There are incidental breeders, small breeders, and large-scale commercial breeders. These are people in the hobby of keeping tortoises who have taken the passion of keeping these animals to the level of reproducing them for fun and, in some cases, profit.

Be aware that not all breeders participate in the reptile shows. Outside of the reptile shows, contact information for these breeders can be found in reptile magazines or on the Internet. The most successful way of finding a good tortoise breeder is by word of mouth and networking.

Among the different levels of tortoise breeders, the incidental breeder is your best opportunity for getting a good tortoise at a good price. The offspring produced by the incidental tortoise breeder are usually the result of a pet tortoise having offspring when the owner was not trying to breed the pet tortoise. It is these babies that usually get the greatest care because they are personal

Marginated tortoises are infrequently bred in captivity.

pets. Another benefit is that the owner is usually not very concerned about the price of the offspring, because they are not breeding as a business. Their main concern is finding a good home for their animals. The only drawback to obtaining your tortoise from this source is finding the person. Obtaining a contact for such a person is almost exclusively by word of mouth and is usually a matter of being at the right place and at the right time.

An easier source to find than the incidental breeder is the small, or backyard, tortoise breeder. These individuals try to have their pets breed as a means to provide supplemental income for their hobby, but their operation is still on a small enough scale to provide individual care for the offspring. These types of tortoise breeders usually advertise in the local tortoise club newsletters, in addition to various bulletin boards on the Internet. They also produce offspring on a more consistent basis. You can still get a good level of service and value, but generally the price of the tortoises will be higher than with an incidental breeder.

Finally, there is the large-scale commercial tortoise breeder. Many of these breeders produce tortoise offspring on such a large scale that it is virtually impossible to provide individual care for all the juvenile tortoises. This might be seen as a bad thing, but this allows the breeder to sell the tortoises at a better price than the backyard breeder. Usually the commercial tortoise breeder has taken a long time to develop their operation and in doing so has also developed a good knowledge base along with a good reputation. Many large-scale breeders have a company name that can be found in the usual informational resources and have their own web sites.

The large-scale tortoise breeder can have some distinct advantages as a source for your first tortoise. As mentioned earlier, they have usually been around for a long time so it is easy to do a background check. Also, they have usually turned their passion for keeping tortoises into a business because they not only like dealing with the tortoises they keep, but they also seem to enjoy the interaction with the new keeper (for the most part).

Selecting The New Tortoise

Once you know where your new tortoise is going to come from, you might wonder what does a good, healthy Russian tortoise look like and how to pick one out of a group.

Wild-Caught vs. Captive-Bred Tortoises

Here we must distinguish between the two types of pet tortoise. One type is wild caught, describing animals that are taken out of the wild. These are also sometimes referred to as wild-collected (WC) tortoises. If a Russian tortoise is described as imported, it is almost certainly wild caught. The other type is captive-born and raised tortoises, sometimes called captive-bred (CB) tortoises. These are tortoises that have hatched from eggs laid in captivity. It is these tortoises that are the preferred pets for various reasons.

Controversial Wild Collection

There is the ethical question of whether tortoises should be taken out of the wild. This is a highly controversial topic. Many of the tortoises you see in the pet trade are wild caught (though the trend is slowly changing toward a higher percentage of captive-bred tortoises) These animals are sometimes collected in vast numbers, possibly having a negative impact on the wild populations. Many people believe this is wrong. If you have strong feelings against the taking of animals out of the wild, don't purchase one. By purchasing a wild-caught tortoise, you are not saving it, but you are perpetuating the market and opening up another slot for yet another wild-caught tortoise.

This is not a clear-cut issue because you cannot have captive-born tortoises without a founding captive population to produce those captive-born offspring. The founding population are the wild-caught tortoises that produce the captive-born tortoises. This is an issue that needs more research from biologists, hobbyists, and policymakers. It is up to you what route of tortoise ownership you choose to take.

Wild-caught tortoises are usually lower in price, but often you end up paying for that lower price in both time and money. Wild-caught tortoises are notorious for carrying a heavy load of internal parasites and other diseases. While they can often live with these problems in the wild, the stress of being yanked out of their natural habitat and thrown into an unnatural environment leads to them being unable to deal with these pathogens. At that point, the WC tortoise's health starts to decline. This is followed by a veterinarian visit with a sizable veterinarian bill and possibly to a dead tortoise. So, any savings you might realize by purchasing the WC tortoise are exhausted, probably along with more money. Wild-caught tortoises often are also more difficult to acclimate to captivity.

It's only fair to mention that there are some minor advantages to acquiring a WC tortoise. Wild-caught tortoises are normally adults, so if you can acclimate them, you will have full-grown adults immediately. If you intend to eventually breed your pets, this can reduce the amount of time you have to wait before the tortoise can breed. Another plus is that you can be relatively sure WC tortoises are not related, which is beneficial for genetic diversity if the final goal is the breeding of your pets.

The best tortoise to acquire is, of course, the captive-born and raised tortoise. The CB tortoise will present the fewest problems and the greatest rewards. The only real disadvantage in obtaining the CB tortoise is the amount of time it usually takes the tortoise to reach maturity, but as mentioned earlier, it is very rewarding to raise that tortoise from hatchling to adult. When obtaining the CB tortoise, you usually don't have the problems that you would with a wild-caught tortoise.

Selecting a Healthy Tortoise

Regardless of where the tortoise comes from, there are certain things to be on the lookout for when actually selecting one. The most important characteristic you are looking for is a tortoise that is active and alert. If you can see the tortoise eating and/or drinking,

You do not want to purchase a Greek tortoise that looks like this. It appears listless and has sunken, half-closed eyes.

those are usually good signs that it is a healthy and well-acclimated animal. You also want to look for signs of dehydration, such as sunken eyes or excessively loose skin around the head or limbs. Looking at the eyes, you want to see the eyes fully opened, in addition to them completely filling the eye socket fully.

The nostrils should be dry and clear. A common problem among tortoises is a runny or wet nose. This can be an indication of many problems, so it is best to avoid any tortoises that have a runny nose. The Russian tortoise and the European tortoises in general are very active by nature. If the temperature is warm and comfortable, you will usually see these tortoises running about in an animated fashion. When the tortoise is picked up, it should again be active and alert. You should have no trouble looking for the above-mentioned indicators. If this is not the case with the animals you are looking at and they are inactive and will not come out of their shell, it is probably a good idea for you to look elsewhere for your tortoise.

Even if you have followed the preceding suggestions it is always a good idea to take your new tortoise for a preliminary vet checkup. Scheduling a veterinarian visit as soon as you bring the new tortoise home is an important step regardless of the origin of the tortoise. Buying a captive-bred tortoise does not guarantee that it is free of problems. Even the most well-intentioned keeper or breeder occasionally has problems that might go unnoticed, so the veterinarian visit is recommended so that any of these small unnoticed problems can be dealt with before they become large noticeable problems. The most important item the veterinarian needs to look for is any form of parasites, either internal or external. These can cause serious problems if they go unchecked. With the conclusion of the vet visit and a clean bill of health, you are now ready to face the basic upkeep of your new tortoise.

Quarantine

The vet visit does not always guarantee your tortoise will be free from health problems. This is why it is always recommended that you quarantine any new animal before adding it to its final home. Any serious health problems should make themselves apparent within the first week or so, but they can take longer to show up. Any parasites discovered during the vet visit can be treated at this time to reduce the chance of spreading the parasites to its permanent home—and any other tortoises you may have. It is recommended that the quarantine period be at least 30 days, with the acknowledgement that the longer the quarantine period the better. If you only have a single tortoise, this is not as critical as it is if you are adding a tortoise to an established group.

Ideally the quarantine area should be similar to the permanent enclosure but located in a different room, although this is not always possible. At the very least, the quarantine area should be a separate enclosure away from the permanent enclosure with a strict hygienic protocol, such as washing hands and utensils when working from one enclosure to the next. Do your upkeep of the quarantine enclosure after performing the chores for any other reptiles you may have.

With its clear and bright eyes and lack of any nasal discharge, this Russian tortoise appears to be perfectly healthy.

Chapter 3

Housing

The most basic consideration in terms of housing your new tortoise is whether the tortoise is going to be kept indoors or outdoors. Outdoor housing is the preferred option; however, this is not always feasible. Some people may live in an area where it is not safe to house a tortoise outdoors, due to the climate or the presence of feral animals. For those people, indoor housing is the only option. For other keepers, the weather for part of the year may be suitable for outdoor housing but not for the rest of the year. Keepers in those situations may opt to house their tortoises outdoors when the weather is good and indoors the rest of the time.

Russian tortoises and the other *Testudo* can be housed indoors or outdoors if the conditions permit it.

Indoor Housing

Once you have determined the tortoise enclosure will be inside, the next thing to consider is the size of the enclosure. While you must give your tortoise plenty of room, bigger is not always better. You would not place a hatchling Russian tortoise in a one acre corral, because you would most likely lose it. More importantly, in such a large area you could not control the environmental conditions. At the same time, you would not place an adult Russian tortoise in a small container the size of a shoebox.

As a general guideline, base your enclosure dimensions on the length of your tortoise. Measure your tortoise across the plastron. To find the length of the enclosure, multiply the length of the tortoise by a factor of ten. For the width, multiply the length of the tortoise by a factor of five. And for the height, multiply the length of the tortoise by three. This can be feet or inches, depending on the size of the tortoise. This gives you a rough idea of how big to make the

Enclosure Size

To figure out the size of the enclosure you will need for your tortoise, you can use this simple formula to determine the minmum space requirements:

length = 10x

width = 5x

height = 3 x

Where x equals the length of the tortoise.

enclosure. As an example, if your tortoise is 5 inches (12.7 cm) long, the length of the enclosure should be 50 inches (127 cm), the width should be 25 inches (63.5 cm), and the height should be 15 inches (38.1 cm). For a hatchling Russian or similar tortoise, some examples that usually come close to these dimensions are 10- to 20-gallon aquaria (38 to 76 liters) (or similar glass enclosures) and plastic sweater boxes. These containers each have their advantages and disadvantages, which will be discussed later in this chapter.

When properly outfitted, plastic sweater boxes make good enclosures for Russian tortoises, especially hatchlings.

Types of Indoor Caging

Glass and Plastic There are many glass enclosures that are made today specifically for use in maintaining reptiles. If you use a glass or clear enclosure, you have to observe the tortoise to make certain it is not always trying to go through the wall, not realizing that a barrier is there. Most tortoises adapt well to clear enclosures, but some do not. It seems vary by individual. If you find that your tortoise is one of those that is always trying to get out, you might be able to remedy this by placing a dark border on the bottom 4 or 5 inches (10.2 to 12.7 cm) of the enclosure. You can use a solid colored tape, or you can paint a border on the outside walls of the enclosure.

Be aware that glass enclosures can retain heat under certain conditions. This can be either an advantage or a disadvantage depending on the ambient temperature. In cooler climates, the retention of heat is an advantage because it makes it easier to maintain a proper temperature

Be Careful of the Sun

It must be mentioned that if a glass enclosure is used, caution must be taken in positioning the enclosure in relation to the sun. With sunlight streaming in, the glass enclosure acts as a heat trap, which can quickly lead to the overheating of the tortoise. A precaution that you can take to avoid this when using a glass enclosure is to use an enclosure that is of adequate size, allowing sufficient air circulation. Good air circulation can also be provided by using an enclosure that has low walls. The best solution is to avoid placing a glass enclosure in an area that receives direct sunlight.

The tortoise table—essentially a large box on legs—is a time-tested method for housing tortoise indoors.

gradient. In a warmer climate, it is a disadvantage because the retained heat can harm your tortoise if the temperatures are not properly monitored and controlled.

Many people prefer to use enclosures made from plastic shoeboxes, sweater boxes, or under-the-bed blanket boxes because of the initial low cost of the enclosure and the easy availability. These types of enclosures can be found in almost any hardware store, discount store, or department store. These types of plastic containers are usually constructed with low-profile sides, so heat is not easily retained, and as a result, there is less chance of the tortoise becoming overheated than in an aquarium. Remember that lack of heat retention can also be a disadvantage.

Both glass and plastic enclosures have the benefit of being waterproof. This means they are easy to clean without being concerned with the enclosure falling apart and rotting. With other types of enclosures—primarily those made of wood—there is the added work of providing a waterproof finish. This is usually going to have to be refinished on a regular basis for proper maintenance. All tortoises need the proper level of humidity. The glass or plastic enclosure makes it easier to maintain that humidity without worrying about rot, mold, or mildew.

Custom Cages While glass or plastic box enclosures can have their benefits, their drawback is that they are usually not very attractive. If you are concerned about the appearance, you should consider a custom-made enclosure. These can be as elaborate as a decorated cabinet or as simple as a tortoise table—essentially nothing more than a wooden box on legs. In the cooler climates, a full enclosure is a more practical choice because it will be easier to maintain the required environment for the tortoise. In a more temperate zone, the tortoise table would be a better choice because retaining heat is usually not a problem in such areas.

The tortoise table has been the enclosure of choice for maintaining tortoises, such as the Greek or Russian tortoises, indoors for well over a hundred years. The enclosure is very basic in design, in that it has the appearance of nothing more than a bookcase that has been laid on its back and the shelves removed. In actuality, this very idea has been employed by many keepers, but it is not recommended because bookcases usually use very thin wood for the backing and, as a floor, this material does not hold up very well to the activities of the average Russian tortoise. If you are the handy type, you can easily build a tortoise table from scratch, using shelving material and 3/4-inch thick plywood. Then again, if you are not the handy type, there are many lumber yards that are willing to cut the wood you need to the specified dimensions for a minimal charge. The lumber yard can also construct the enclosure for yet another minimal charge. Then they can also finish the enclosure for still another minimal charge. By now it should be pretty clear that you can save yourself a good deal of money by completing as many steps of the building process yourself as you are able. If done properly, this can actually be part of the fun of tortoise keeping.

Buying a Custom Cage

Some enterprising craftspeople have decided to take advantage of the growing popularity of the reptile hobby by building and selling beautiful custom-made enclosures to hobbyists. These enclosures are designed to be functional and aesthetically pleasing. The builders generally are willing to build a cage suitable to the particular species you are keeping. The cost of such a cage will be many times the cost of building one yourself, but for the less-than-handy hobbyist, buying one may the best option.

Companies and individuals that custom-make reptile cages can be found at herp expos, in reptile related publications, and on the Internet. You can also contact a local carpenter and find out if he or she would be able to build a cage to suit your needs.

Ideally, the table should be constructed of a hardwood, such as oak or oak veneer. A table made out of hardwood will last the lifetime of the tortoise, if it is properly constructed. The only problem with this is that any hardwood is going to be expensive. Pine is a good and less expensive alternative. Pine must be properly finished because of its softness. Particle board is less expensive but is not recommended. If it is not sealed properly, it tends to fall apart when it is exposed to moisture. When considering the flooring of the enclosure, it is a good idea to construct the floor of plywood because it is much more durable than solid pine. It also allows you to provide a flatter surface for easier construction.

The sides of the tortoise table can be constructed of standard width pine boards, depending on the height of the sides that are desired. A good height for the sides would be 12 inches (30.5 cm), which should be tall enough to provide a good layer of substrate in addition to keeping a Russian tortoise from escaping. The 12 inches mentioned is only intended as a suggestion, and you can always make the walls higher if you deem necessary.

Once the tortoise table is constructed, the next step is to provide a protective coating to the surfaces of the floor and walls. As a covering you can use a veneer, a laminate, or a liquid coating, such as paint or plastic. A solid covering, such as the laminate or veneer, is much more durable than a liquid covering but is also much more difficult to apply. If not applied properly, it will actually do more damage than good because it tends to trap moisture under the surface. One of the easier durable coatings to apply is polyurethane, which is a type of liquid plastic. Polyurethane does tend to be soft, but if enough layers are applied carefully, it can last for many years. A suggested course of action would be to sand the interior of the enclosure to a very smooth finish and then apply 10 to 15 coats on the inside. Also apply three to five coats on the outside. This might sound like a great deal of work and time, but each coat dries in roughly 30 to 60 minutes in 70° to 80°F (21.1 to 26.7°C) temperatures. Allow the finish to dry for a day or two to be sure the polyurethane is totally dry (even though it might seem sufficiently dry a few hours after the last coat). You now have a tortoise table that is almost ready for the addition of your new Russian tortoise, but before you can add the tortoise you have to decide on a substrate and any additional furnishings.

A Greek tortoise housed on hay, one of several substrate choices for *Testudo* enclosures.

Substrates

At the very least, the substrate you provide must supply your tortoise with a decent footing. You can use anything from newspaper to gravel. Some commonly used substrates are sand, soil, sand/soil mixture, pine bark mulch, cypress mulch, aspen bedding, and many kinds of hay or grass clippings. These substrates can be used alone or in combination with each other to add variety to both the appearance and the environment the tortoise is exposed to.

Russian tortoises as well as many of the other *Testudo* come from harsh environments with a surface of rock and sand. It is for this reason that a substrate of rock and sand seems appropriate for their setup. The tortoises are well adapted to their rough habitat and actually seem to enjoy this kind of setup in captivity. Regardless of the substrate that you do decide to use, be sure that it is free of any kind of chemicals or contamination, such as animal waste. This is mentioned because it is not uncommon to use substrates or rocks that you would find outdoors to furnish your enclosure, and this is perfectly acceptable. You do have to be careful and be certain the material is clean. If using loam, leaf litter, sand, or dirt from outdoors, try and collect it from areas that are well drained. Also, try and collect it from areas where the chance of the substrate being exposed to animal wastes or chemicals, such as fertilizers or chemical runoff, is unlikely. Some examples of chemical runoff would be oil, gas, and automobile coolant.

Many of these substrates are readily available at any hardware store, garden supply center, pet store, feed store, or landscaping outlet. Purchasing the substrate will eliminate any concern you might have about collecting material that might be tainted. Unless you can be completely sure that the area you are collecting substrate from is free of contaminants, you should purchase it instead of collecting it.

Substrates and Impaction

It is commonly believed that some substrates, such as sand, soil, gravel, and some mulches, pose a risk of gut impaction. Impaction of the digestive system occurs when the tortoise ingests something that blocks the digestive tract, so the tortoise can no longer digest or pass its food. The tortoise eventually suffocates or the gut ruptures due to a buildup of fluid and food that it cannot pass. Why tortoises ingest the substrate is a topic of much debate. However, it is believed that if all of the environmental conditions are correct and the tortoise is well fed and well hydrated, impaction is of little or no concern. It may help to feed the tortoise its food in a dish or on a flat rock or piece of cardboard to avoid accidental substrate ingestion. If you are keeping a careful eye on your tortoise and he is acting normally, there is little reason to be concerned.

Cage Furnishings

The Russian tortoise's habitat often consists of rough and rocky terrain. They are well adapted to this habitat, so it is good practice to provide structure, such as rocks or logs, for the tortoise to climb on or go under. Not only is it aesthetically pleasing to set up the enclosure in this manner, but it aids in the stimulation of the tortoise's natural behavior and leads to better overall health. Russian tortoises like to dig tunnels or burrow down when provided with the opportunity. In an indoor enclosure, this is not always practical because the shallowness of the enclosure usually prevents having a layer of substrate deep enough for burrowing.

You can provide tunnels using flat pieces of stone, such as slate or flagstone. Be sure that the support structure is stable and strong enough so it does not fall or tip over and injure the tortoise. Whenever you provide any kind of structure that the tortoise can climb on, try to place the furniture in such a manner that if the tortoise falls off and over on its back, it is not in danger of overheating or drowning (if the structure is near the heat lamp or water bowl). Anytime there is structure that the tortoise can climb on, there should be low structures or a substrate that the tortoise can get a grip on that will aid the tortoise in righting itself if it should end up on its back.

Water Bowl

Although Greek tortoises and other *Testudo* are adapted to arid habitats, they require access to fresh water at all times.

Be sure to leave space for a water bowl. It is highly recommended that a water bowl filled with clean water be available at all times.

Russian tortoises are not heavy drinkers, but it is always better to give them the choice to have the water or not. When choosing a water bowl, be sure to select a dish that is shallow enough for the tortoise to at least reach into, although it will usually climb all the way into the bowl, if it is able. The dish should be heavy so the tortoise does not knock the bowl around, spilling the water and making a mess. A good dish for this application is a plant pot saucer. If you go this route, be sure to get a glazed dish for ease of cleaning.

You might want to consider keeping more than one dish on hand. This saves you some time washing bowls, which the tortoise will dirty quickly. The plant pot dishes are inexpensive, so it will not cost prohibitive to buy several to keep on hand. These dishes can be found in the same places where you would purchase the substrate.

When first placing the bowl be sure the tortoise is using it. In the beginning, you can place the bowl in a corner so when the tortoise is exploring its enclosure, it is sure to run into the dish. As time goes on, you can move the bowl away from the corner, so the tortoise is not always walking through it. The tortoise should know where to find its water.

Heating and Lighting

With the enclosure all set up with the necessary furnishings and water, there are a couple of final considerations with indoor housing: heating and lighting. These two topics are related but not the same.

Heating and Temperature Tortoises are reptiles, and as such, they are dependent on their environment to provide a body temperature that allows them to maintain their normal bodily functions and metabolism. Tortoises have adapted to use the range of temperatures in their habitat to maintain their metabolism. It is for this reason that a temperature gradient is required for these tortoises in captivity.

Behavioral Thermoregulation

Because tortoises and other reptiles have no way of controlling their temperature physiologically, they use various behaviors to do the job. This is called behavioral thermoregulation, which simply means controlling temperature through behavior. For tortoises, behavioral thermoregulation involves moving in and out of the sunlight as they get too hot or too cool. The keeper needs to be aware of behavioral thermoregulation in order to set up a proper captive environment. The tortoise must be given a range of temperatures in his enclosure, so it can select the temperature it prefers at a given moment.

Tortoises select different temperatures based on different needs. The tortoise will seek out warm temperatures when it is preparing to go out to forage and feed. It will then seek out a cooler temperature when it is bedding down for the evening. For most of the *Testudo*, a temperature range of 75° to 95°F (23.9 to 35°C) seems to be acceptable. This means one end of the enclosure should be around 75°F (23.9°C) and the other should be near 95°F (35°C). At night, the temperatures for the whole cage can stay at the low end of the range, 75°F (23.9°C).

When you observe your tortoise, you should see that it moves close to and then away from the

Wild Mediterranean tortoises regulate their body temperature by moving in and out of patches of sunlight.

heat source throughout the course of the day. If it is staying far away from the heat source all the time, the range is most likely too high. On the other hand, if it is spending all its time directly under or on top of the heat source, the range is probably too low. Buy two accurate thermometers and put one on each end of the habitat to keep track of the temperature. The digital thermometers sold in electronics stores are the most accurate ones. Set the thermometer so that it is reading the temperature at the same height as your tortoise's shell.

There are two basic categories of heat sources. There is the overhead heat source and there is the underneath heat source. The most common overhead heat sources are the ceramic emitter and the incandescent lamp. The incandescent lamp produces heat as a by-product of producing light, and the ceramic emitter gives off heat from an electric current being passed through a resistive coil embedded in a ceramic core.

The wattage of the lamp or emitter is going to determine the amount of heat produced. A higher wattage is going to produce more heat. The wattage you will need is dependent on the temperature of the area where the enclosure is placed. You will need a higher wattage heat source if you live in a cooler climate area or you keep the temperature of your home on the low side and a lower wattage heat source if the opposite is true. Also, the wattage will depend on the size of the enclosure. It will take more watts to heat more space. The only way to be certain as to how much heat you are going to need is to set up the enclosure and measure the temperature over the course of a few days. This is another reason to have the enclosure completely set up before getting your tortoise. If you buy the tortoise and then set up the enclosure without measuring the temperature beforehand, you may subject your pet to temperatures far outside of its preferred range.

The incandescent light is a good source of daytime heat because it provides a natural basking spot, but it is not a good heat source at night. What many keepers do when heat is required through a 24-hour period is to use the ceramic emitter during the night and an incandescent lamp during the day to provide a day-night cycle indoors. This is easily accomplished by having two fixtures, one with a ceramic emitter and the other with an incandescent light. You can connect each of these to separate timers set on whatever light cycle you choose.

The other method of providing heat is to provide that heat from below. Most keepers use a device called an undertank heater. This is a plastic mat with a resistive conductor embedded inside. These mats are usually placed under the enclosure or substrate. This type of heat source should be used with caution because they have a tendency to overheat if there is not enough air circulation. This problem can be overcome by making sure there is space between the mat and the enclosure or by using a thermostat to adjust the power on an as-needed basis. The heat mat can also be used as an overhead heat source in the tortoise's retreat by securing the heat mat to the ceiling of the enclosure and making the ceiling low enough for the radiant heat to reach the tortoise.

Regardless of what type of heat source you use, it should be placed at one end of the enclosure to give you a maximum temperature gradient. It may sound like an easy enough task to maintain a good temperature range, but what many keepers do not realize is that the temperature in the tortoise's area will change depending upon the temperature in the area surrounding the enclosure. This can lead to problems with the changing of the seasons if there is not a thermostat set up to regulate the temperature for the tortoise. One of the warning signs to look for is the tortoise refusing food.

Heat Carefully

Ceramic heat emitters, high-wattage bulbs, and high-intensity bulbs (such as mercury vapor lamps) produce tremendous amounts of heat for their size. To avoid creating a fire hazard, you should not use these bulbs in regular plastic sockets. Instead, use ceramic sockets that are designed to handle the heat that these bulbs generate. You can find ceramic sockets at hardware stores and sometimes in the reptile sections of pet stores.

When supplemental heating is added—as is usually necessary during the winter—you should note that this tends to lead to an increase in dehydration through increased evaporation. Even in regions with high humidity, this is a concern because the local environment of the enclosure will dry out. The tortoise then runs the risk of becoming dehydrated due to the increase in the loss of body fluid through respiration. Keep a careful eye on the humidity level in the enclosure and make sure the water bowl is always full of clean water.

Lighting and Photoperiod

Lighting has only been mentioned as a source of heat up until this point, but lighting also makes it pleasant to view the tortoise in addition to providing cyclic cues for the tortoise's behavior. There are also special fluorescent bulbs and mercury vapor lamps that provide ultraviolet light—specifically ultraviolet B waves (UVB)—which is essential for the natural metabolism of calcium. This point will be covered in greater detail in the section on feeding. At this time, the beneficial effect of this lighting is speculation for the most part, but many tortoise keepers use them just to be on the safe side.

Access to natural sunlight is one of several benefits to housing your tortoise outdoors.

The lighting should be set up on a 12-hour cycle but can be varied if a simulation of the seasons is desired. (This may be important for breeding.) The lighting can be mounted over the tortoise table by using wooden studs to form an arch over the table, and the lighting can be mounted to that directly or hung from the arch. Another method of hanging the lighting is to use PVC tubing, such as that used for plumbing. You can construct the arch using normal plumbing fittings for the angles, and you can attach the arch to the table using pipe brackets. Be sure to use tubing that is of sufficient size and thickness to support the light fixtures. For fluorescent lighting, you can use a single or double light strip mounted directly to the arch. In some instances, you might have to suspend the light strip using chains in order to get the light closer to the tortoise.

Why Outdoors?

There are a number of reasons why outdoor housing of tortoises is usually better for them than indoor housing. The primary benefit of outdoor housing is the exposure to natural sunlight, which contributes to calcium metabolism and stimulates natural behaviors. Also, there is the space. Outdoor enclosures can be much larger than most indoor ones. This increased space gives your tortoise more exercise and more of an ability to act as it would in the wild. You have more options for landscaping in an outdoor enclosure. In particular, you can grow plants for food, cover, and appearance right in the enclosure.

Outdoor Enclosures

Early on in the section on housing, it was mentioned that outdoor housing is the preferred method when keeping tortoises. While many people are limited to keeping their Russian tortoise indoors, there will be those of you who will be fortunate enough to be able to house your tortoise outdoors for at least part of the year, if not full time. You are going to have the same basic considerations as you would with an indoor enclosure. You will also have the added consideration of furnishing the enclosure with plants, which is very difficult to do in an indoor enclosure.

Size

The size of the enclosure is probably the most important factor to think about. An area that is 6 feet by 10 feet (1.8 by 3 m) is sufficient enough to house one to six Russian tortoises. You can go beyond these dimensions, but you have to be careful to keep it to a size that is manageable. If too large an area is provided, it becomes difficult to keep track of your pets. This is especially true if the enclosure is well planted. Be aware that Russian tortoises are fantastic escape artists. They are not only great at digging, but they are also wonderful climbers. With indoor enclosures you can control this fairly well, and even if they do escape indoors, your

Even if you house your tortoises indoors, you can make a temporary outdoor cage to give your tortoises some sunlight and foraging time.

Position your enclosure so that it receives direct sunlight for most of the day, but provide your tortoises with shady areas.

chances of finding them are pretty good. Outdoors, this is not the case. You would be very surprised at just how far these animals can travel in a given day. It is for this reason you should make the enclosure a manageable size.

Location

When locating the enclosure, try to place the enclosure in an area that receives plenty of sunlight. If the enclosure receives full sun throughout most of the day, you then have the option of adding plants and shelters to regulate the amount of sun the tortoises are exposed to. After all, it is the exposure to the sun that is the most important reason to house your tortoise outdoors. When keeping Russian tortoises outdoors, make sure they are kept in an area that is dry and well drained. Russian tortoises seem to get sick quickly if conditions are allowed to become cold and damp. This is mentioned here because when you house your Russian tortoise outdoors, you have to make sure the soil in their enclosure is well drained and allowed to dry out between waterings and occurrences of rain. If you have soil that drains poorly, you are going to have to add sand, gypsum, or gravel to increase the drainage.

Construction

The task of constructing a barrier is the next project. There are several materials you can use, depending upon how much work, time, and money you wish devote to it. The easiest material to use is 16-inch-wide boards (40.6 cm) fastened to stakes that are sunk into the ground at each corner. A 12- to 24-inch (30.5 to 61 cm) chicken wire skirt should be fastened to the bottom of the boards and buried to prevent the tortoises from digging out. This is just a basic idea using basic concepts. The idea is to provide a wall that the tortoise can not climb over and a underground barrier, so that the tortoise cannot dig under the wall. Some tortoise keepers have gone to the extent of digging out the enclosure, installing a layer of wire mesh, and replacing the substrate on top of that in order to prevent the great escape. This seems to be extreme, but in some instances it is warranted.

Wood If you decide to build an enclosure using wood, you will need to seal and finish the wood, so it does not decay. There is also treated wood that is used for decking and yard furniture. Using treated wood is not recommended unless you are certain that the treatment used is nonhazardous. Many governments require manufacturers to disclose the treatment used and any hazards they present to people. If it is hazardous to people, it is probably hazardous to your tortoise.

There is also a new material that is currently available that is a composite of wood and plastic. It seems to be the ideal material for this application, but it is extremely expensive and has not been on the market very long. This type of wood is sold for decking and lawn furniture and seems to be quite durable. It is cut and formed as if it were wood and does not need to be finished. Because it is manufactured for decking, the size of the boards available is limited.

Bricks and Blocks There are other durable materials you can use such as cement block, brick, concrete, or chain-link fencing, each having its

Fences

If you house your tortoise outdoors, you may want to fence in your yard. Having your enclosure in a fenced-in yard has several advantages. If your tortoise manages to escape from the enclosure, it will now have to get through the fence. This may give you the time you need to find your pet. Fencing helps keep out wildlife that could harm your tortoise. Additionally, it helps discourage anyone from coming in your yard and stealing or harming your tortoise. While most people wouldn't do that, there are those that would.

advantages and disadvantages. The cement blocks, similar to cinder block, are a good choice if you can afford the wasted space of the 6-inch-wide blocks. The blocks are still going to have to be buried, as would any enclosure wall, into the ground at least one block deep. You can use cement to attach the blocks, or you can fill the blocks with dirt and add trailing or vining plants to the top. The plants make for an attractive cap to the wall, and when the roots grow into the wall they provide the support that holds the wall together. Some advantages of this type of enclosure are that it is easily disassembled and moved or expanded

Extending the enclosure walls into the ground will prevent your tortoise from digging out underneath, like this Hermann's tortoise has done.

Cinder blocks make for an attractive and sturdy tortoise enclosure—in this case for spider tortoises, *Pyxis arachnoides*.

on. Cinder blocks are usually not very expensive either.

In all actuality, any type of brick would make an attractive enclosure. When using bricks other than cinder blocks, it is necessary to properly cement the bricks in place, which requires a good deal of time, skill, and money. Once it is constructed, this is probably the most durable of all the enclosures. Before constructing any wall, it is a good idea to dig a trench and fill a portion of that trench with a layer of gravel. It provides a good foundation for the brick wall, and for the other types of enclosures, it allows for good drainage, which reduces rotting.

Chain-link Fence A less expensive but equally durable enclosure material is the chain-link fence. Even better than normal chain-link, there is a type of link fence called tennis court fencing, which is used for tennis courts or sports courts in general. This type of fencing has one-inch (2.5 cm) mesh and is usually coated in plastic, which comes in green or brown so you can color coordinate your yard. The plastic coating not only adds a little style but it also helps in reducing corrosion of the metal. The one-inch mesh makes it more difficult for tortoises to climb the fence while allowing smaller tortoises to be housed in the pen without the worry of the tortoise fitting between the links as with a standard large mesh. This type of enclosure is usually permanent in construction because the corner posts are set in cement for a good foundation for the fence.

The fencing itself is probably going to have to be special ordered from a fence outlet, but all the posts, rails, attaching hardware, and other materials can be easily found at any of the major hardware stores. You will also need gravel and cement to set the posts, and you can find those materials in the same stores.

A nice feature of chain-link fencing is that it does not provide a solid barrier. From an aesthetic point of view, it presents a more open and less enclosed look. The chain-link fence is also durable and will last the life of the tortoise. There are two main disadvantages, which are easily overcome. The first disadvantage is that the tortoise can see to the other side. Some animals will constantly try to get through the fence—like some tortoises kept in glass enclosures. This situation can easily be remedied by placing strips of plastic through the links. These are made specifically for the purpose of preventing a clear view through the fence. These plastic strips are available at the same locations as the chain-link fencing itself. It is suggested that the strips be cut only to the height of the fully extended tortoise to preserve that open view while still restricting the view of the tortoise.

The second disadvantage is that a Mediterranean tortoise, especially a Russian Tortoise, can climb the fence. Yes, your tortoise is that good of a

An enclosure made of chain-link fence can last the lifetime of your tortoise.

climber and escape artist. They are usually limited to climbing up the corners of the enclosure. To prevent this you can use sheets of galvanized steel or 6-inch-wide (15.2 cm) strips of plastic (normally used for lawn edging) secured to the corners, so the tortoise cannot get a foothold. If constructed properly, this kind of fence will not only look good but will last a lifetime.

There are other materials you can use, which are only limited by your imagination. With the previously listed examples, the possibilities you can come up with are really endless. There are several points that must be consistent no matter what material you use:

- The material needs to be weather resistant.
- The materials must not pose a hazard to your tortoise.
- The walls of the enclosure need to be buried deep enough to prevent the tortoise from digging out.
- The walls must be high enough to prevent the tortoises from climbing out.

Remember that the walls of the enclosure do not have to be very high. The most practical height is high enough to step over, yet not so low that the tortoise easily climbs over. A height of 16 to 24 (40.6 to 61 cm) inches above ground level is a good height for most tortoises.

Soil

Once the enclosure is constructed, it is a good idea to prepare the soil for growing plants before adding any structure in the enclosure. Ideally, you should have the soil tested for its nutrient content and how well it can support plants. This can usually be done at the county agricultural office for little or no charge. They also usually provide suggestions for any deficiencies they find in the soil. You then want to add mulch and manure, making sure to till the mixture in properly. It is also a good idea at this time to add some kind of soil conditioner, such as sand or gypsum, to break up any hard compacted soil and provide better drainage. It should also be noted that some species (i.e., the Egyptian tortoise) should be kept in a dry environment because they cannot tolerate humid conditions.

Hide Boxes

A number of materials can be used as hide boxes and shelters. You are limited only by your imagination and the safety of your tortoise. For outdoor housing, the shelter must be able to withstand the elements. Here are some ideas:

- Wooden or plastic box
- Shelter made of cinder blocks and a roof
- Hollow log
- Small garbage can
- Top of a cat litter pan
- Large clay or PVC pipe

This Hermann's tortoise has a nice shed for a shelter, but you can use something less elaborate, if you wish.

Shelter

With the enclosure constructed, the next step is to provide a hiding area that will allow the tortoise to escape the elements. The hide must be in an area that is well drained. Remember that Russian tortoises cannot tolerate cool and damp conditions. The key is to make sure they are always dry. With this in mind, the hiding area especially should be dry and well drained. If you don't have well-drained soil you might consider removing the soil under the hide to a depth of roughly 1 foot (30.5 cm), replacing the soil with sand or gravel, and placing the hide on top of that. Once that is done, a bed of hay or some other soft substrate is a good finishing touch for the inside of the hide.

The hide can consist of something as simple as a wooden or plastic box to something as complex as a small house or shed. The decision on what type of hide you use will depend mostly on the average temperature the tortoise will encounter. In warmer climates where the evening temperatures do not get below 50°F (10°C), a small hide such as a wooden box, flat stones on brick supports, or even cinder blocks placed on their side and partially buried will suffice as a hide for the tortoise.

In areas where the temperatures dip below that level, a hide with supplemental heating is required. Supplemental heating can be provided in the same manner as indoor supplemental heating, but you must make sure the heat source and the power to the heat source is well protected from the weather. It is a good idea to provide a ground fault interrupt in the power circuit to prevent electrocution of the tortoise and yourself. This is a device similar to a circuit breaker that monitors current flow in two wires and can be bought at any hardware store. If the current in one wire should vary, the circuit opens.

Some common heat sources that are used for outdoor enclosures are heat mats and ceramic heat emitters. The emitters can be mounted on the ceiling of the hide or even mounted on the wall. The placement of the heat source should be towards the rear of the hide for the best efficiency. Be careful the tortoise cannot be burned by the heat source.

For larger hide areas, a heat mat or pig blanket is recommended. These are plastic mats that are intended to provide a warm area to farm animals. They are manufactured to be weatherproof, but the connection for the power is not. Take the precaution of covering the connection, so that it is waterproof. These heat mats come in many sizes and can be purchased at many pet stores and animal feed stores. They can also be ordered online. When using the heat mat outdoors, the mat should not be totally

Russian tortoises are good climbers and seem to enjoy having rocks to climb in their enclosures.

covered. This will not only increase the risk of fire but may reduce the life of the mat.

Regardless of the heat source, using a thermostat or timer is a good safety precaution. With a thermostat, you can set the heat source to come on when the outside temperatures dip below a comfortable level. If the heat source is allowed to produce heat constantly, there is a chance that the tortoise can overheat, not to mention that it is a waste of energy. If it is necessary to use a heat source, it is also a good idea to cover the opening of the hide with a material that allows the tortoise to come and go as it pleases. You can use something as simple as an old towel tacked over the door (you can add layers depending on how cold it is). You can also use a swinging door similar to a doggy door. It is advisable to paint the door a different color than the hide to distinguish the door from the walls of the hide box.

Water

Once again, the introduction of water cannot be overemphasized. Even in an outdoor enclosure that gets watered on a regular basis, a water bowl is highly recommended. As with the indoor enclosure, a glazed flower pot saucer makes a great water dish. You can sink the dish into the ground so the lip is about a 1/4 inch (2/3 cm) above ground level. A 12-inch (30.5 cm) diameter dish makes a good-sized dish, and that would be considered a minimum size needed for a water bowl in an outdoor enclosure. The water should be changed daily to every other day. This task is made easier by using the spray blast of a water hose to remove the old water and decreasing the pressure to refill the dish. Not only does this make removing the dish unnecessary, but the water that is removed waters the plants.

When providing water for the outdoor pen you are not limited to the use of a dish. You can also make a cement water catch in the shape of a pond or stream. Be sure to properly seal the cement to prevent the leaching of any chemicals from the concrete and also to prevent the concrete from crumbling. These types of water dispensers can look great in an outdoor enclosure and are no harder to service than the ceramic dish.

Plants

Which plants you use for your tortoise enclosure will depend on your climate and what is available at your local gardening stores. In most places, there will be hundreds you can choose from. The following list provides only a few suggestions.

- **Ficus**
- **Grape**
- **Hibiscus**
- **Lavender**
- **Mulberry**
- **Rose**
- **Rose of Sharon**
- **Waxleaf**

Furnishings and Plants

With all the environmental fixtures in place, it is now time to add any structures, such as rocks or logs, and plants that you want. These items are important in that they seem to make the enclosure bigger by breaking up the open space. If you have a single tortoise, this provides them with something to occupy them by forcing them to go around, over, or through the structure. If you have more than one tortoise, the structures also provide visual barriers in the event that there is any aggression between two or more tortoises. The visual barriers will allow the line of sight of an aggressive or pursuing tortoise to be broken. A tortoise is easily distracted, so when the line of sight is broken, the aggressive tortoise usually gives up pursuit.

When placing these visual barriers, you want to try and use up as little actual floor space as possible. The idea is to provide barriers that the tortoise can use, such as tunnels and logs that are leaned and raised against another structure. Be careful to make sure any raised structure is securely in place, so there is no danger of the object falling and crushing any of the inhabitants of the enclosure.

At this point you can choose to add plants or not. If you choose not to add plants, you will see that over time, the local vegetation will find its way into the enclosure. This is sometimes the better way to go, because the first plants that usually colonize a vacant piece of land are the broadleaf weeds and grasses. These can serve as good forage material for the tortoise.

To actually compile a list of the types of plants you could use to add to the enclosure would fill a very large book in itself. It is for this reason the discussion on the plants you can use will be presented in general terms. When providing plants in the enclosure, try to keep in mind that the plants are going to grow. Try to envision what the plants will look like in a year from the time you planted them. The point is that you want to provide enough space for the plants to grow.

Invaders

Occasionally, keepers have problems with the local wildlife. If this is the case, you might have to provide a fully covered enclosure. Once again, the key is to observe your animals an see if they are going to need added protection. Watch to see that the tortoises are not being picked on by the local animals, and that the tortoise beds down in a secure place for the night. If you do see a problem, the added protection can be something as simple as a wire mesh cover, or you might have to provide something as complex as a walk-in structure, depending on what type of animal is threatening your tortoises. Common culprits are coyotes and dogs, rats, raccoons, and crows.

As mentioned earlier, grasses and weeds are going to establish themselves, so the plants you want to provide are those that are going to provide shade or cover and, secondarily, food. Plants such as hedges, small bushes, and even some small trees are good for this because they are slow growers—for the most part. If you treat them as if they were bonsai and keep them trimmed to a small size, they can become a pleasant addition to the enclosure, as well as being a functional part of the contained ecosystem.

When selecting the plants for the enclosure, it is good practice to select plants that are not toxic. This is not as critical as you might imagine because there are many plants that are toxic to mammals that are not toxic to tortoises. Also, tortoises seem to know what they can and cannot eat, provided that they are not starved and do have a choice. For your own peace of mind and to be on the safe side, refrain from using any plants that you have questions about. To find out if a plant is toxic or not, you can consult the nursery where you bought the plants. You can also inquire about the plants in question at the biology department at you local museum of natural history or any major college or university. Searching through the many lists on the Internet to find any plants in question usually yields very good results.

When selecting plants also try to obtain plants that might be useful outside of providing shade and cover. Selecting plants that you know to be edible is a good practice. There are many books available that list edible plants including trees and shrubs. More on this will be discussed in the section on feeding and nutrition.

Housekeeping

If you are keeping your tortoise under optimal conditions with a good supply of food, you are going to get optimal output, which usually requires daily cleaning. When using newspaper as a substrate it is a good idea to change the paper every day or two. With a more natural substrate, such as sand or soil, it is easy to do a daily spot-cleaning by using a scoop or dustpan to remove any dirty substrate. Outdoor enclosures are maintained in a similar fashion by picking up the waste with a scoop on an as-needed basis.

You will occasionally need to do a more thorough cleaning of an indoor enclosure. Remove and dispose of the substrate and clean the enclosure, furnishings, and food and water bowls with a disinfectant. A solution of 5 percent bleach in water or a commercial disinfectant is recommended. After cleaning, rinse thoroughly and allow the enclosure to dry out completely before adding new substrate.

Chapter 4

Feeding and Nutrition

ussian tortoises and the other *Testudo* are primarily herbivorous. This seems simple and at first glance, but the simplicity of the idea is deceptive. Factoring in all the various species of plants you can feed your tortoise adds complexity to this issue. Also, be aware food and water will be of no use if the tortoise cannot process or metabolize the material. This is mentioned here because it is an important point that seems to be taken for granted by many keepers. If you don't provide your tortoise with adequate temperature and lighting, nutritional problems will arise regardless of the nutritional content of the diet.

The Basics

The Russian tortoise is dependent on its environment to maintain its body at an adequate temperature to digest the food it consumes. When keeping tortoises, this is a key point, because if a sufficient temperature is not maintained, the tortoise will starve to death, regardless of the availability of food and water. If the tortoises are too cool they won't eat, but if they are too warm, food passes through too quickly without being completely digested. It is for this reason that you should take a little time after you have your tortoise set up and observe it in the enclosure. You are going to have to establish the balance that will work for your situation. The balance that you are looking for is a combination of food, water, temperature, and humidity that will support normal activity and growth.

Temperature and Digestion

In the housing section, the importance of heat and hydration was mentioned in several places. The reason they are stressed so strongly is because it is these two components that permit the metabolism to proceed properly, allowing the tortoise to thrive in captivity. It is also the area of husbandry in which keepers most often fail to provide adequate conditions for their tortoises.

> Temperature strongly affects a tortoise's digestion and metabolism, and keeping your tortoise too warm or too cool can cause digestive problems.

Be aware that there are not only differences among the different types of tortoises, such as the Russian tortoise and various other species of *Testudo*, but there are also going to be differences among individual tortoises. This is why it is important to try and provide as much of a choice among all the housing components as you possibly can. The temperature is the most important component. By providing a temperature range of 75 to 95°F (23.9 to 35°C), you are giving the tortoise the ability to select a temperature based on its needs at the moment.

The Russian tortoise has developed several adaptations to its harsh environment. If the temperatures should drop too low, the tortoise will stop eating and go into hibernation. In the wild, this usually coincides with the unavailability of plants and food that occurs during that period. It also allows the tortoise to survive the season when the temperatures are too low for the tortoise to process or digest food. In the summer, there is the opposite extreme; the temperatures climb so high that there is the possibility that the tortoise can overheat. During the periods when the temperatures are that high, the tortoise will seek out a cooler refuge estivate until favorable conditions return.

In nature, the tortoise usually has enough energy reserves (in the form of fat and other stored nutrients) to survive both states of inactivity and fasting. In captivity, if the tortoise is forced into either of these situations and it does not have sufficient reserves, the tortoise's health will suffer. With this in mind, the importance of a good temperature range should be quite clear.

Natural Diet

After establishing an adequate captive environment, the next task is to provide the food and nutrition. It is common practice when keeping tortoises in captivity to try and provide as natural diet as possible. This is a great deal more difficult than it sounds, because the only way you are going to know exactly what the species eats in the wild is to observe many tortoises over the entire range over many years. Then, you have to obtain the very foods the tortoises have been consuming in nature, which can be difficult. With the Russian tortoise, because of the region of the world they come from, it can be hard to find the native plants.

In the natural habitat, the tortoise has an immense variety of plants, insects, and other foods to choose from. Again, this will vary on a seasonal and regional basis. It would be impossible to offer this variety to a pet tortoise. To overcome this obstacle, you aim to provide a substitute diet that has been successfully used on captive tortoises by others. The main diet of these animals in captivity is the result of trial and error by many keepers over many years.

Browsing vs. Grazing

In the wild, the Russian tortoise and the other Testudo have a feeding style that biologists call "browsing," as opposed to "grazing." Browsers are animals that feed on leafy greens and berries for the most part. Grazers are animals that feed almost exclusively on grasses. The Russian tortoise is not an avid grazer. These tortoises feed mainly on leaves, but sometimes feed on mushrooms, insects, and carrion. These last items comprise a minor part of their diet. This makes them opportunistic feeders, but the majority of their diet is leafy greens.

Components of Nutrition

There are four major components to good tortoise nutrition: fiber, protein, vitamins, and minerals. It is the balance of these major components--in addition to the balance of heat and hydration--that will keep your tortoise in good health. The easiest way to approach this without becoming a nutritionist is to provide as much variety as you possibly can within the boundaries of the tortoises natural preferences.

Russian tortoises are browsers. Because we know this, we really don't have to know the specific plants on which they feed. All we have to do is provide a variety (as much of a variety as possible) of leafy greens to fulfill the nutritional needs.

Many tortoise keepers make the mistake of focusing on specific components. If you focus on any one specific component, it will most likely result in an overage or a deficiency in another component. This is mentioned because there is an overemphasis on individual components, such as feeding a low-protein/high-fiber diet, in the general tortoise literature. This came about in reaction to the old practice of feeding dog and cat food to the family pet tortoise in the past. This usually leads to a severely deformed tortoise that is in all likelihood in bad health.

Through the years, we have discovered that this is not a good diet for these particular tortoises. It would seem that the digestive system is not adapted to process the fat and animal protein that dog and cat foods contain. You can think of a tortoise as a bunny with a shell. Rabbits have very much the same feeding habits as tortoises. The major difference is that the tortoise is dependent on its environment to provide the energy to process its food.

Digestion

Tortoises are hindgut fermenters with a very similar digestive tract to the rabbit or horse. The stomach is very crude and not much digestion actually takes place in the stomach. Most of the digestion process takes place in the large intestine with the aid of bacteria and other microorganisms. Because much of digestion takes place in this modified large intestine, a good amount of food is only partially digested before the next step in the process, elimination. This is important because the tortoise's digestive system has evolved to be very efficient with what few nutrients it is presented with. You should also keep in mind that most tortoises, including the Russian tortoise, are probably not exclusively hindgut fermenters. Nutrients seem to be taken in by the stomach and small intestine, also. This theoretically gives them at least some ability to digest animal proteins.

All species of *Testudo* need a varied, plant-based diet. A varied diet composed of mostly leafy green plants is best for them.

In the wild, it would appear that tortoises are almost constantly eating during periods of activity. However, most of the foods they are eating are so nutrient poor they almost have to eat constantly in order to obtain sufficient nutrition to survive, grow, and reproduce. You can see how these animals have adapted to survive in harsh environments.

If you look at protein, fiber, minerals, and vitamins individually you will be able to have a

Coprophagy

Occasionally you might see your tortoise consume its own feces. While this might be an unpleasant sight, this is mentioned here because it is a common practice among tortoises and is thought to be an important part of tortoise nutrition. If you remember, the Russian tortoise is a hindgut fermenter, and many nutrients are wasted because of this. It is suspected that consuming its own feces, called coprophagy, is a means of reducing the waste of available nutrients. It is like running the food through the digestive process a second time to absorb those nutrients made available when the material was broken down the first time around. Tortoises of many species will even consume the feces of other animals, both in nature and in captivity.

better understanding of how they fit together. Keep in mind that there are other components, but these four are the major components of the tortoise diet that deserve particular attention. If these components are in balance, the others components will fall into place, assuming you provide a varied diet.

Protein

Protein is the most important component in nutrition, because it is the major physical building block of all life. In simple terms, a protein is made up of a fixed number of specific molecules called amino acids. The sequence in which the amino acids fit together and the shape of the structure that is formed by the combinations of these acids determines the type of protein you have. Proteins not only form structural building blocks, but they also provide specific functions—as catalysts, chemical messengers, and more—in the internal processes of all living things.

From this description it should be clear that protein is probably the most important factor in nutrition. It is also a poorly understood part of tortoise nutrition. This leads to many misconceptions. Excess protein is blamed on many physical problems in the development of tortoises. The problem with this line of thought is that it is really not known that protein is the actual culprit, because it is also not known how much protein is required and how that protein is processed in tortoises. Much of the available nutritional information is based on models created for mammals. While this is the only starting point we have, it does not take into account that tortoises are ectothermic, nor the metabolic demands of the shell.

There is a common belief that too much protein is bad. This is probably true, but too much of any one thing is bad in the diet of any animal and leads to an imbalance of other components. The problem with this line of thought is that when we think of protein in tortoise nutrition, we really do not know what too much is. Protein is a very necessary component of nutrition for the proper development of any living creature, but as far as tortoise nutrition goes, we really

Dietary Mysteries

There has been little research on the nutritional needs of reptiles, even less on the needs of herbivorous reptiles, and even less than that on the nutritional needs of tortoises. There is much we don't know about the diet, digestion, nutrition, and metabolism of *Testudo*. For most dietary components, we really don't know how much is too much or too little. The best way to overcome this lack of accurate information is to provide as much variety as possible and not fixate on any one food item.

don't know the actual requirements. The only thing we can do is to give the tortoise a choice and hopefully provide enough of a variety to obtain the proper balance.

Russian tortoises are mostly herbivorous. The main source of protein should come only from plant material. As was mentioned earlier, these animals are hindgut fermenters, so the amount of protein that they actually obtain from their natural forage is minimal. For this reason, the actual protein content of any plant should not be a concern if the plant is part of a varied diet.

Marginated tortoises seem to eat more animal matter than the other species, but they still eat a mostly herbivorous diet.

Animal protein should not be fed because animal protein is usually associated with fat. Some experts believe that the fat is the real problem and not the protein, although the animal protein could very well be the problem, considering that the tortoise's digestive system has developed to deal with very nutrient-poor plant material. You will see that this is yet another controversial topic for which there is little hard data to base decisions on. With this in mind, it is probably safer and healthier to focus on plant material as your primary source of protein, again making certain to offer as much variety as possible. If you

Macro and Micro

There are two major categories of nutrients, the macronutrients and the micronutrients. The macronutrients make up a majority of the bodyweight and include protein, fat, carbohydrates, and water. The micronutrients are the vitamins and minerals, such as sulfur and zinc, among many others, that compose a small portion of the actual makeup of the body. Both macronutrients and micronutrients are essential for the normal cellular processes, and without them, the tortoise will not thrive.

Dietary Do's and Don't's

While many aspects of tortoise nutrition remain uncertain, there are few definite things you should and shouldn't do when feeding your tortoise.

Do

- provide a plant-based diet
- feed as wide a variety of plants as possible
- feed mostly leafy green plants
- provide a suitable calcium supplement

Do not

- feed animal protein, like dog or cat food
- feed a lot of fruit
- offer spoiled or moldy items

notice that the tortoise does consume the occasional insect or animal matter, there should be no cause for alarm as long as this does not become a staple of the tortoise's diet.

Fiber

The next important component in tortoise nutrition is fiber. In mammals, fiber serves the function of retaining moisture and aiding in digestion. In tortoises, this is also the case, but it does more, as it is at least partially digested with the aid of beneficial bacteria in the hindgut. For the most part, fiber is considered the indigestible plant material that is consumed by the tortoise. The common belief is that you want to feed a high-fiber and low-protein diet. In actuality, you want to feed a balanced diet. Once again, variety in the diet is the key. There are so many unknowns that the only way we can get around them is to provide as much choice to the tortoise as possible.

Fiber, or roughage, is also reported to aid in keeping the parasite load down in tortoises in the wild. If you are maintaining your tortoise or tortoises outdoors, this is something that should be considered. No matter how diligent you are in maintaining a parasite-free area your tortoise will pick up internal parasites, and the roughage will usually keep the parasite load to a minimum.

Vitamins

Vitamins are the next important component in nutrition. Vitamins are minute components that are essential in aiding the normal biological processes in the body but are usually not produced by the body. They do not themselves produce energy or serve a structural purpose, but they are important for normal bodily functions. Any deficiency in a vitamin will lead to a deficiency disease. If you are supplementing certain vitamins in certain forms, you can create a poisoning situation, or toxicity from having too much of a given vitamin (referred to as hypervitaminosis).

This sounds simple, but it only demonstrates again how little is actually known about vitamins in living organisms. We know that vitamins are required in a specific ratio. We also know that different species require different vitamins in different ratios. We know a little about what tortoises require, but it is once again based on mammalian models. In the end, what this means is that we really don't know for sure what the vitamin requirements for tortoises are.

There are many vitamin supplements available, and the only way to be certain that any of them are any good is to try them and observe the results you obtain with your tortoise. It is recommended that you start with those that have been around the longest time and have a noteworthy reputation among tortoise keepers. Talk to other keepers and look at the results that they have achieved. If you are feeding the recommended varied diet, there should be little need for vitamin supplements, but it is advisable to use a vitamin supplement once a week or so to be on the safe side. Over time, if you see you are obtaining the results you are looking for with only the foods you are feeding, then you can omit the supplemental vitamins altogether. There will be more information on supplements later in this chapter.

Russian tortoises and other Mediterranean tortoises spend much of their time foraging.

Other Minerals

Calcium and phosphorus are definitely the two most important minerals for tortoise keepers to understand. However, there many other minerals tortoises need to maintain their health. These include iodine, zinc, potassium, and many, many more. Most of the minerals you need, your tortoise needs, too. Trying to keep track of all these minerals is a fruitless task. The best way to be sure that your tortoise is getting the minerals it needs is to feed the widest variety of plants possible and provide the recommended supplementation.

Minerals

The final major component of a nutritious diet is minerals. Minerals are basic elements that make up a small portion of the actual structure of the body, but they are extremely important in providing structural material and also providing regulatory mechanisms for normal metabolic processes. One of the most important sets of minerals in tortoises are calcium and phosphorous. Both of these minerals are of equal importance, because it is the interaction of these two minerals that regulate each other. The body uses these two minerals in the ratio of one to one. For every one unit of calcium, you need one unit of phosphorous. This sometimes becomes a problem because a tortoise's diet is naturally high in phosphorous. A recommended dietary ratio is a minimum of 2:1 of calcium: phosphorous. If you focus on one and not the other, you are almost certain to lead to an imbalance which, in turn, is most likely to lead to other health problems. You can obtain the suggested ratio by feeding calcium-rich plants and supplementing calcium in the diet.

Calcium Calcium is the one mineral that is recommended to be supplemented at every feeding. The most easily attainable and usable form is calcium carbonate. This form—if used in conjunction with natural sunlight--is very difficult to overdose, which is why it is recommended. (See the section on supplements for more information). The calcium ion is widely used in many bodily functions including muscle contractions, nerve impulses, bone structure, and activation of enzymes, among other things. This is why calcium is so important.

There is an optimal level of calcium in the bloodstream that the body tries to maintain. When this level drops below the acceptable range, the thyroid gland releases one hormone that stimulates a release of calcium from the bones while also increasing calcium retention by the kidney and, with the aid of vitamin D, also increases the uptake of calcium by the intestines. When the level of calcium in the bloodstream reaches the acceptable level, the thyroid gland releases a different

Hatchlings and Hydration

Lack of hydration, leading to problems in calcium metabolism, seems to be a common problem with hatchling Mediterranean tortoises. Because of their small size, hatchlings dehydrate very quickly. Time and again, there are reports of hatchlings that fail to thrive and have soft shells. It is suspected that the actual cause of this failure to thrive is kidney failure due to dehydration, which in turn affects bone development. Proper hydration is critical to the health of baby tortoises. This point cannot be stressed enough and will be discussed further in the chapter on tortoise health.

hormone that signals the kidney and intestine to reduce calcium uptake and at the same time encourages the deposition of calcium in the bone. This is a simplified version of the process, but it is sufficient for the average tortoise keeper.

The involvement of the kidneys in this process is one reason hydration has been stressed in preceding sections. Anything that stresses or harms the kidneys, such as dehydration, will effect calcium metabolism detrimentally. Some keepers assume that because these tortoises come from desert habitats, they receive all their water through their food. In the wild this might be the case, but they also have control of their microhabitat, which, in all likelihood, they select to reduce water loss.

Housing your tortoise outdoors allows it to obtain much of its own food.

Feeding Your Tortoise

Nutrition is the area in which most, if not all, keepers have the greatest difficulty. It is also the area in which there is the greatest amount of confusion and controversy among tortoise keepers. In the following paragraphs, some of the more troublesome points will be addressed so that the guesswork can be reduced to a minimum.

In the wild, tortoises are mainly opportunistic feeders. The available food is determined by what plants are available in the home range and at a given time of the year. These animals have adapted to harsh environments where plant life can be sparse. In response, they have adapted to eat almost anything. Therefore, it is up to you to try and regulate what is available to the tortoise.

If you are lucky enough to maintain the tortoise outdoors, the tortoise will be able to forage and choose what it wishes to eat. If you can allow this, you have the opportunity to see what the tortoise selects. Many keepers are able to keep their tortoise outdoors at least part of the year. It is during this time that the most valuable information is provided to you, if you observe the tortoise's behavior.

Always try and let the tortoise tell you what it needs or likes. If you can allow the tortoise to forage outdoors, watch the plants it consumes. Unless the tortoise is starving, it is only going to consume the plants that are appealing to it. It must be mentioned here that not all plants that tortoise's consume are edible to mammals. If a plant is poisonous to you, it may not be poisonous to the tortoise. With that said, you shouldn't allow your tortoise to consume plants that you know to be poisonous. To some extent, you can

Plantains (the yellow and green stalks) are one of many common yard plants that make good forage for Mediterranean tortoises.

trust your tortoise to know what it can and cannot consume. If the tortoise is not starving, it will pass on the plants it does not like and move on to the ones it does. From this you can get an idea of what exactly to feed your tortoise, if you cannot allow the tortoise to forage outdoors all year.

Plants to Feed

Weeds and Wild Plants
The Russian tortoise is a browser. It normally consumes leafy greens. This can include all those nasty weeds that come up in a lawn. Lawns, open fields, empty lots, school grounds, and city parks are all excellent hunting grounds for finding a good variety of natural fare for your tortoise. You can even grow your own, if you so choose—even indoors, you can grow a few pots of a couple species of plants. There are many companies that sell seeds for many of the weeds that are acceptable food for your tortoise.

The list of the available plants that you can feed is virtually endless, but your best source of specific information is going to be a book on the local edible plants of your area. To give you a starting point and an idea of some of the more common plants that are usually consumed by many tortoises, including the Russian tortoise, a list follows.

- Chicory
- Clover
- Dandelion
- Mallow
- Plantain and other plantagos
- Thistle
- Wild mustards

Cautious Collecting

If you harvest food plants for your tortoise from parks, school grounds, the yards of your neighbors, or other areas away from your own yard, be sure that the owners of those areas do not spray any chemicals on the plants. Chemicals such as insecticides, weed-killers, fertilizers, and others can be harmful or fatal if consumed by your tortoise. Many city parks spray to control mosquitoes and caterpillars. Check with your local park commission to find out if your municipality sprays. Also, collecting from roadsides is not a good idea. The plants are often contaminated with motor oil, gasoline, and antifreeze.

There are many others, as well. What you want to focus on is any broadleaf green that is seasonal. These are usually the plants that pop up after a rain and die off after a few months. The leaves are usually very thin. It is in the springtime when they are the most abundant, but as you

Your local produce department will have a wide variety of greens you can feed to your tortoise.

move closer geographically to the equator, the winter becomes the prominent season for these plants. Again, keep in mind that your tortoise is usually not picky and there are not many plants that pop up in the spring that are harmful. If you have any question as to if a plant is suitable or not, your local museum or plant nursery is usually a good source to confirm any suspicions you might have.

Watch your tortoise and it should tell you what is good for it or not. If the tortoise is not starving, it will usually not consume any plant that is bad for it. If the tortoise does take a bite of a plant and you see the tortoise spit it out, it is usually a good idea to remove the remainder of the plant and any similar plants in the area, just to be on the safe side.

When you are collecting plants away from your own property it is a good idea to know the practices of the groundskeepers of the areas you are collecting from. You want to be certain that pesticides or any other chemicals have not been used. Schools and public parks are usually a safe bet because of the presence of children, but it is also a good idea to monitor an area that you are interested in collecting from to see if chemicals or any evidence of chemicals are being used. Collecting plants from the roadside is usually not a good idea because of the emissions from automobiles that settle on and are absorbed by the plants.

Most of the previously mentioned plants produce flowers, fruits, and berries. These items can be fed, also. If you do feed fruits, feed them sparingly. Remember that the Russian tortoise has adapted to feed on dry items, so very moist items should be avoided. Many of these items can be dehydrated and stored during the periods that they are not growing. The plant can be rehydrated or fed dry on an as-needed basis. Be careful to keep it dry to avoid spoilage. If the material does get moldy, it can make your tortoise sick.

Woody Plants While broadleaf weeds seem to be the primary source of food for the Russian tortoise, it is by no means the only source. The Russian tortoise will also feed on the leaves that fall from trees, shrubs, and bushes. Some trees, shrubs, and vines that can be planted for cover and forage material in a *Testudo* enclosure include mulberry, grape, ficus, rose, hibiscus, and Japanese waxleaf—a plant poisonous to people but harmless to Mediterranean tortoises. Many other types of landscaping plants are also acceptable.

Grocery Produce In your quest to provide maximum variety to your tortoise, remember your local grocery store. When picking out plants from the produce section, try to focus on the leafy greens. If you are providing as much variety as possible, there are no restricted items, for the most part. The only caution is to be careful not to overuse beans and related plants, if at all. These have been implicated in some nutritional disorders.

Some of the more commonly used items are any of the lettuces (iceberg is low in nutrients, however), kale, escarole, endive, romaine, collard greens, mustard greens, spinach, and turnip greens. Non-leafy vegetables including squash, shredded carrot (and tops), broccoli, sweet potatoes (shredded), beets (shredded and include the tops), and okra are good to rotate into the

Variety Is Key

Many different dietary deficiencies are found in Russian tortoises and their kin, but most of them seem to be caused by a simple problem. Many keepers tend to feed a very limited range of foods. Also, some keepers feed inappropriate foods. These are two simple problems to overcome. It is now well known that if an adequate variety of the tortoise's natural fare is provided, nutritional deficiencies are virtually eliminated. This can be easy if you keep an open mind. All plant material is fair game to consider in a tortoise's diet.

Cultivating Cactus

Pear cactus, *Opuntia* sp., is a calcium-rich plant and good addition to your tortoise's diet. It can be found in well-stocked supermarkets and specialty grocery stores, as well as in the arid areas of North America. You can also grow it yourself, as this cactus is easily propagated. Begin by cutting a pad along the seam at the bottom of the pad where it attaches to the main plant. Allow the cut to dry out for a day or two, and then plant the pad in a 1-to-1 ratio of a soil and sand mixture. Plant the pad with the cut end just below the surface. Water regularly but allow the surface to dry between waterings. In a few months, you will have a good supply of cactus to feed your tortoises—and yourself.

diet once in a while. Fruits such as apples, pears, and berries can also be fed to add to the variety, but high-moisture fruits such as melons should be avoided. Remember to mix up the menu items as much as possible.

Prepared Diets

As the hobby of keeping tortoises grows, commercial products made just for tortoises are making their way onto the market. There are many vitamin/mineral supplements and even packaged foods. Many of these items are of questionable value, and those products usually come and go fairly quickly. There are also some products that have been around for a while, and they do make providing good nutrition for your tortoise easier. There are several packaged diets that seem to be very well formulated and beneficial. These are yet another route you can choose to increase the dietary variety. When selecting one of these diets, try to speak to as many keepers as you can that have used or are using the diet.

There is one caution when using some of the grain-based diets. There are some diets that seem to be very nutritious. When these are fed to the Russian tortoise in excessive amounts, it can lead to very rapid growth. Whether this is a good or bad thing is yet another topic of much debate, but it can be controlled by reducing the amount of food given. If any of these diets are used in feeding the Russian tortoise, you should limit offering it to once or twice a week.

Supplements

This is another one of those controversial topics because there have been few independent

Pear cactus makes a nutritious food for tortoises and is fairly easy to grow.

studies of supplements in reptiles. All good supplements are based on a biological model. These models are usually based on warm-blooded animals. References for a reptilian model are impossible to find. In one study on reptiles, the most complete supplement was shown to be Centrum, a supplement made for human consumption and available at grocery stores and pharmacies. Because of this, the only supplement I recommend is Centrum, although there are some newer herp supplements on the market that seem to be very good. Centrum must be pulverized before adding it to the food.

As mentioned earlier, calcium should be supplemented on a daily basis. One of the easiest sources of calcium to obtain is calcium carbonate. This can be found in the form of a powder or as a solid in the form of cuttlebone. Cuttlebone is the internal skeleton of a squid-like creature, the cuttlefish. It has been used as a calcium supplement for birds for many years. The cuttlebone can be fed whole or ground up into a powder. When feeding calcium carbonate, it is important to remember that the body does not process calcium without vitamin D3. This can be obtained as a supplement, or the body can produce the D3 in the skin when exposed to ultraviolet B waves of

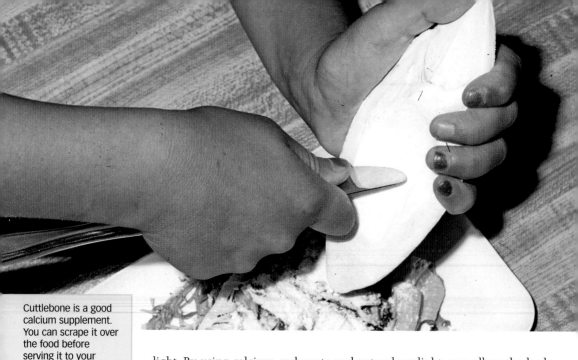

Cuttlebone is a good calcium supplement. You can scrape it over the food before serving it to your tortoise.

light. By using calcium carbonate and natural sunlight, you allow the body to regulate the calcium naturally. When vitamin D3 is used as a supplement, there is the added risk of overdosing the calcium, which can lead to calcium being deposited in the tissues and joints of the tortoise.

Feeding Amount and Schedule

Once you know what you are feeding your tortoise, you may be wondering how much and how often you should feed your tortoise. In nature, when the tortoise is active it is usually feeding, but if you remember from the notes in the natural history section, they are not active often in their harsh habitat. Also, the foods they are feeding on are usually nutrient poor. For this reason, development is slow, and overfeeding is not a concern. In captivity, your tortoise is given ideal conditions, so its feeding schedule is going to be quite different than what you would expect to find in nature.

You can feed every day if you feed a limited quantity. If you are feeding mostly fibrous, low-nutrient plants, such as weeds and grasses, overfeeding shouldn't be a problem. The only time you might be presented with an overfeeding problem is if you are feeding a rich or nutritious diet, such as most items in the produce department. In this situation you would want to limit the quantity you feed.

Vitamins A and D

Usually keepers are concerned with making sure they give their tortoise enough of each nutrient and are not worried about giving them too much. In the cases of vitamins A and D, there is some cause to worry about oversupplementing. Both of these vitamins are fat-soluble, which means they collect in the fat tissue of the body. When too much builds up, there are detrimental effects. Just about any vitamin or mineral can be oversupplemented and cause a toxic reaction, but it seems the happen most often with these two vitamins.

To avoid oversupplementing vitamin A, it is best to provide vitamin A in the form of beta carotene. The body turns beta carotene into vitamin A as it needs it, usually preventing vitamin A from reaching toxic levels. Beta carotene is found in leafy greens and red and orange vegetables; better vitamin supplements contain it instead of regular vitamin A. To avoid oversupplementing vitamin D, use a calcium supplement that contains no vitamin D. Your tortoise should get all the vitamin D he needs from the sun. If you house your tortoise indoors, use supplements sparingly and provide the correct lighting.

You should notice that your tortoise is most active in the morning and in the late afternoons. These are usually good times to feed to be sure the tortoise has the opportunity to eat. It is also a good idea to scatter or hide the food to encourage activity and browsing. You should not be too concerned if your tortoise ingests a little substrate with its food, as long as the substrate does not have any sharp edges, such as splinters, or the tortoise does not ingest the substrate directly as if it were food. If you are using a grass or hay substrate, this is not a concern at all. Leaving the remains of leafy greens in the enclosure is not a problem, as long as the material does not stay wet and rot. Russian tortoises seem to actually enjoy foraging on dried greens. All other uneaten food should be removed once the tortoise has retired for the day.

Chapter 5

Breeding and Reproduction

Many tortoise owners strive for that ultimate
validation of their tortoise-keeping endeavors.
That validation is, of course, the reproduction of
their tortoises. A great many factors need to come
together under the proper circumstances to
provide success in that final goal. You first need the proper
environment, matched with a good diet to provide healthy
animals. Then, you have to be certain that you have a male
and a female of breeding size. Hopefully, this pair will be
compatible. With any luck, they will breed, and with a
little more luck, they will produce eggs, and with still
more luck, the eggs will be fertile, and even still with just a
little bit more luck, the eggs will hatch to give you some
nice healthy offspring. So you see, there is a great deal of
luck involved. There are certain things you can do to
increase your chances of success, and those will be
discussed here.

Starting Out

Starting out with captive-bred young tortoises increases your chances of success for breeding. A wild animal develops patterns feeding, breeding, and other behaviors based on the environmental cues in its habitat. When you take an animal out of that environment, it is sometimes very difficult to change those patterns. Therefore, to breed wild-caught tortoises, you will usually have to exactly mimic the environmental conditions they are used to—a difficult task. The only disadvantage of starting with captive-bred young tortoises is that you have to raise them from hatchling to adult and that will take several years, although the feeling of accomplishment is much greater when your raise babies to breeders.

The size of a tortoise determines if it can reproduce or not more than the age does. Your tortoise can reach breeding size in as little as five years, if you provide an ideal mix of diet and environment. However, this is not recommended because if breeding is the goal, a change of seasons should be provided, which will slow down the growth process. It is still not known if an accelerated growth rate has any detrimental effects on the long-term health of tortoises. With this in mind, you can expect your tortoise to reach breeding size in about ten years. During that time, you can set up a seasonal cycle that your tortoise will hopefully use for its own breeding cues.

In marginated tortoises and most other *Testudo,* the males (left) have a concave plastron and the females (right) have a flat one.

Breeding Size and Sexing

A breeding-size female Russian tortoise is approximately 9 inches SCL, which is the Straight Carapace Length. This is the straight-line, end-to-end measurement taken along the centerline of the bottom of the shell. The male is mature at a length of approximately 5 inches SCL. Both sexes will get larger than this, but this is an approximate minimum adult size.

At this size, the sex of the

To Breed or Not to Breed?

Although the current trend in the herp hobby is for hobbyists to breed their animals, you should not feel like a failure if you don't breed your tortoises. Not everyone can be a breeder and not everyone should try. You should only attempt to breed your tortoises if you have carefully considered all that is involved in the project, including what you will do with the baby tortoises. Without a plan, you could end up stuck with a few dozen growing tortoises to feed and house, or have a breeding pair that did not survive hibernation, or other problems. Think carefully before jumping into tortoise breeding.

tortoise is easy to determine. A male is usually smaller than a female of the same age, but the most obvious distinguishing factor is the length of the tail. The male Russian tortoise will have a very long tail, as compared to the female. The Russian tortoise is also unique from the other forms of *Testudo* in that both the male and the female have a flat plastron. In the other *Testudo*, the females have a flat plastron and a short tail, and the males have a concave plastron and a long tail. In most species of *Testudo*, the male is usually more elongated than the female, which tends to be rounder in shape. This is not the case in the Russian tortoise, in which both sexes are equally round in shape.

Breeding Behavior

If you have raised your own tortoises from hatchling to adult and you have a sexual pair, there is a good chance that you have already witnessed breeding behavior in the form of ramming and mounting. These behaviors are usually precursors to breeding, but they have been observed in juveniles and same-sex pairs, although the function at that age is not quite clear. Some believe it is a display of dominance. The behaviors can become very violent, with the male biting and ramming the female. The aggression can escalate to such a level that blood is drawn. If you are not prepared for this, it can be unnerving.

Russian tortoises are unlike the other species in that the male (left) has a flat plastron, like the female does.

In some species of *Testudo*, such as the marginated tortoise, mating aggression has resulted in the death of many tortoises in captivity. In the Russian tortoise, this behavior does not typically reach such an extreme. Such behavior is usually seen in a male trying to subdue a female, but it is not restricted to male/female interaction.

Two males in the same enclosure can become violent toward each other. Under these circumstances, it most likely is a contest of dominance or territoriality. When two males combat, it can sometimes lead to the death of one of the combatants. Such aggressive behavior is why visual barriers in the enclosure were recommended. Once the line of sight is broken, the aggressive tortoise normally loses interest. This can also occasionally occur between two females. The violence between females housed together does not normally reach the level of intensity that the male/male or male/female interactions do.

If one tortoise is flipped over by another and the one tortoise cannot right itself, it can lead to the tortoise's death if the tortoise is trapped under a heat source or is in the water bowl. Care must be taken to reduce the chance of this situation by providing visual barriers and to provide a substrate or structure that allows the tortoise to right itself.

Intervention

If the violence between your mating pair escalates to the point that one of them is getting injured, you must be prepared to separate them. This means having another suitable enclosure on hand. Additionally, you may have to seek veterinary care, if the injuries are severe.

Breeding Cues

If your tortoises are housed outdoors, aggression, mounting, and other courtship behaviors can be triggered by the onset of rain, a change in barometric pressure, or a sudden change in temperature. These are some of the cues that trigger this type of behavior. These cues would be difficult to duplicate in an indoor enclosure, which is why there seems to be greater breeding success with tortoises kept outdoors. Some other cues that are suspected to trigger breeding behavior are a lack of food availability, drought followed by rain, and cool weather followed by warm weather. If you separate the sexes for a time and then reintroduce them, there may be an increase in breeding activity. One important cue is hibernation, which can be brought on by any of the previously mentioned variables.

Hibernation

Many believe that hibernation is one of the most important cues to breeding. It is believed that the change in temperature leads to a change in hormones in both the male and female tortoises.

However, many tortoises will breed and produce viable young without hibernation.

When the trigger to hibernate is activated, it can be difficult to reverse. It is therefore a good idea to be prepared to deal with hibernation if it becomes necessary. There are a few key points. The tortoise must have sufficient body reserves to survive the long winter nap, yet it cannot have any food left in its stomach that might rot. The tortoise must also be maintained at a temperature that is low enough that its metabolism does not use up those reserves that it has. Finally, the humidity has to be high enough to prevent dehydration, yet not be so high that the environment promotes respiratory problems. The best suggestion is to keep it simple. If the tortoise is maintained outdoors, your main concern is to maintain the temperature above freezing. A good range is 35° to 45°F (1.7° to 7.2°C), with somewhere in the middle of that range being the ideal.

In the case of the Russian tortoise as well as the other *Testudo*, it is also important that the tortoises do not get wet during hibernation. The usual problem is the substrate being composed of clay or other poorly draining material. This can be solved by providing a hibernaculum (a sheltered area to hibernate in) where the tortoises can safely hibernate.

In the northern latitudes, this can be achieved by providing an area that stays in the above-mentioned temperature range and has good drainage. In very cold climates, the hibernaculum can be built in a greenhouse or close to the foundation of your house. The idea is to provide an area where the average temperature remains close to the required range. One common method is to provide a hole below the expected frost line. Again, be sure there is adequate drainage. The hole is then filled with leaves and grass clippings. As long as the tortoise can dig below the frost line, it will choose the level it needs and the worry is out of your hands.

The tortoise will usually go off feed as the days get shorter. Its metabolism will slow down when this happens, and it will naturally evacuate the remaining contents in its digestive system. The tortoise will then bury down for the winter. This is unnerving for most tortoise keepers.

Hibernate Carefully

When a tortoise hibernates, it goes for several weeks to months without food. During that time, it is using its bodily stores of fats and minerals to survive. A tortoise that does not have sufficient fat reserves can become sick and even die during hibernation. Also, if a tortoise is not in perfect health, diseases and other conditions can become more serious during hibernation. Only put your tortoises through hibernation if they are in peak condition. If one of your tortoises is underweight or not in top health, it is best for the tortoise if you wait for the following year to breed and hibernate, after solving the health issues.

However, it is also the best method because as long as a safe hibernaculum is provided, the majority of the control falls with the tortoise. Keep in mind that the tortoise's actions are going to be triggered by an average temperature and possibly the duration of daylight. Increasing ground temperature will trigger the tortoise to emerge. That does not mean a warm winter day will bring the tortoise out of hibernation because the average temperature of the ground changes gradually.

Another commonly used method takes a little more control away from the tortoise and places it with you. Many keepers will restrict feeding and remove supplemental heating with the onset of cooler temperatures. When the tortoise becomes sluggish, it is placed in an insulated box, which is then placed in a cool area, like a garage or basement. Any cool place will do, as long as that temperature range is maintained. This can also be achieved by placing the box outdoors, as long as the temperatures do not go below freezing. Keep in mind that the more control you take onto yourself, the more there is a chance of something bad happening until you get a feel for exactly what environmental cues the tortoise is keying on to.

Mating

In the wild as well as in captivity, mating usually takes place in the spring and continues through the early summer. It can occur almost on a daily basis. When the animals are ready to mate, you will see the male mount the female from the rear with his front legs on the top of the female's shell. His neck will be outstretched with his head above the female's head. The male will often open his mouth and let out a grunt, but in the case of the smaller species it sound like anything from a gasp of air to a cooing similar to that of a dove. They can be very vocal during the actual mating process.

Greek tortoises mating. The male tortoise can be quite loud during breeding.

Remember that just because you see breeding, it does not necessarily indicate that you are going to get fertile eggs. The female first has to be ovulating at the time. The male has to be not only successful in copulating but must also be fertile. The chance of fertilization occurring from a single mating is not very high. This is why it is difficult to predict when you can expect eggs after mating. Of course, the greater the frequency of copulations, the greater are the chances of obtaining fertile eggs. After mating has occurred, you can expect the female to lay fertile eggs at any time from one to five years afterward. This is because females can store viable sperm for quite some time.

Egg Laying

The eggs are normally deposited in the fall or in the spring if the tortoises are kept in a climate similar to that of their natural range. If the tortoises are maintained indoors or they are kept in a climate that is warm all year, they can deposit eggs at any time of the year. Once they do start depositing eggs in a particular climate, they usually develop a pattern that remains fairly consistent.

Right before a gravid (pregnant with eggs) female is ready to deposit eggs, she will become restless. She will pace the perimeter of the enclosure more than usual. She will walk, sniff the ground, walk some more, and sniff the ground again. This ritual will continue until she finds a nesting sight that meets her liking. Why they choose a particular nesting site is not really known, but many times once a nesting sight is chosen, the same tortoise will choose the same general area

The setup for a nesting box for a Mediterranean tortoise includes a light, substrate, and crumpled newspaper for cover.

year after year. On occasion, the tortoise will choose the very hole in which she deposited eggs the previous year. This phase of breeding presents its own set of unique problems depending on whether you are keeping your tortoise indoors or outdoors.

Indoor Nesting

If you are going to keep your tortoise indoors full time, there are a few options you have for providing nesting sites for your tortoise. The easiest method is to provide a thick layer of substrate that will allow nesting throughout the enclosure. This way the tortoise has a choice of nesting spots. If this is not possible, you can provide a nesting box that can be placed in a hole cut into the bottom of the enclosure so the edge of the nesting box is flush with the substrate. Alternatively, the nesting box can be placed in the enclosure with rocks or ramps leading into the box to allow the tortoise to access the nesting box.

One other option is to provide a temporary enclosure specifically for nesting. Any deep-sided box can be used for this. When a tortoise is observed pacing, she should be watched closely for when she actually tries to nest. You can tell this by the tortoise backing into a corner or up against a structure and digging with her back legs. At this time, the tortoise can be carefully moved to the temporary nesting enclosure.

Regardless of what method you use for an indoor nesting site, you want to provide a substrate that is soft enough to allow digging and moist enough that the hole does not collapse. The substrate must be warm enough to make it appealing for the mother tortoise. Heat can be provided by placing a spotlight roughly 12 to 24 inches (30.5 to 61cm) above the substrate. The nesting box can actually be placed near the basking area that the tortoise normally uses. If a temporary nesting enclosure is used, a clip-type lamp attached to the side facing inward makes a good heat source.

Inside the nesting box, it is recommended that you provide a structure to simulate a bush or shrub. You can use an actual dried bush or shrub, or you can also use shredded newspaper that has

Clutch of Egyptian tortoise eggs laid in a nesting box with a sand substrate.

been wadded up into a loose ball. Another structure you can use is a mound of grass or hay. Mediterranean tortoises will normally use such structure to hide or nest under. If you are using a temporary nesting enclosure, when you shift the tortoise from its normal home to the nesting box, you can cover the tortoise with that structure and the tortoise will usually continue nesting. If the tortoise does not continue nesting, allow a day or two before moving her back to her normal enclosure.

The substrate in the nesting box should have sufficient depth for the tortoise to dig a hole deep enough to deposit and cover the eggs. The eggs must be completely covered and not in danger of being damaged. The

Preparing for the Eggs

Since it is difficult to know when to expect eggs, it is best to have the nesting site available sooner rather than later. As soon as you notice any pacing the cage, sniffing the ground, or digging in the substrate, you should supply a nest site. If you do not provide a nesting site when the female needs one, she may scatter the eggs around the cage or lay them in the water bowl. In either situation, the eggs are unlikely to survive. The female may instead retain the eggs, a condition that can be life threatening.

depth of the substrate should be as deep as the tortoise's outstretched leg is long, plus at least an inch more.

Dirt and sand make good nesting substrates. They must be moistened enough for the cavity holding the eggs to retain its shape. The tortoise normally digs a flask-shaped hole in which to deposit the eggs. A moist substrate will allow this. You are not limited to these substrates because if the tortoise is in dire need of depositing eggs it will do so regardless of the substrate. On occasion, a gravid tortoise will not even nest, but deposit the eggs wherever she desires. These eggs are usually infertile but should be treated as fertile eggs, just to be sure they are not wasted in the event they are fertile.

While many reptiles tend to lay their eggs at night or in the early morning, this is not the case with the *Testudo*. The majority of the time, these tortoises nest in the afternoon. This is not a hard and fast rule, but it does give you a time to be most alert for nesting.

Outdoor Nesting

If you are maintaining your tortoise outdoors, the task of finding the eggs becomes more difficult. If you do not actually see the tortoise lay the eggs, it is almost impossible to find the nest. After laying the eggs, the tortoise will cover the eggs and pack the earth down on top of the eggs. She will then scrape the ground and move surrounding debris over the nest. Many times, the tortoise will also move away from the nest and scrape the ground in an area some distance from the actual nest. This gives the appearance of another nest. When the tortoise is finished with the entire process, the nest totally blends in with the surrounding area. Some keepers avoid this situation by moving the tortoise into a nesting box when they observe nesting behavior. They then remove the eggs and return the tortoise to the outdoor enclosure on completion of the nesting process.

Collecting the Eggs

If the tortoise is caught nesting, you have the choice of allowing the tortoise to finish nesting or collecting the eggs as they are dropped. Collecting the eggs is recommended because the eggs are sometimes cracked when they are dropped into the nest. If collecting the eggs is not possible, the tortoise can be moved after she has deposited the eggs. The tortoise will usually display the odd behavior of continuing the nesting action regardless of where you move her. You can also choose to allow the tortoise to complete the nest, and then dig up the eggs later when she has moved on.

Digging up the eggs must be approached with extreme care. The soil is usually wet and very packed down. As a result, it is easy to damage the eggs while trying to remove the substrate from around them. It is also recommended that tools not be used to remove the substrate from the nest for the same reason. Once you find the nest, it is a good idea to dig around the nest and approach the eggs from the side. This will allow the earth to fall away from the eggs as you approach them which, in turn, decreases the chances of cracking an egg.

When removing the eggs from the nest, try and keep the eggs in the same relative position in which they were found. This is not imperative if you remove the eggs as soon as they were deposited but becomes important if the eggs were allowed to develop for any length of time. If allowed to develop and then moved, the yolk of the egg may move and crush the embryo.

It is always good practice to mark the top of the eggs, which can be done with a soft leaded pencil. It is also good practice to keep a record the number of eggs laid in addition to the date and time the eggs were deposited. Add to that any other information that you might think would be helpful for future reference.

Post-laying Care

Producing and laying eggs takes a lot out of the mother tortoise. After egg laying, she will be tired and probably dehydrated. Make sure she has plenty of nutritious food and water immediately after nesting. You should feed her slightly more food than normal for a few days after laying. With tortoises housed outside that can forage for their own food, you may want to supply a few feedings of nutritious greens for added nutrition.

Most *Testudo* can produce from one to nine eggs in a single clutch, depending on the size and species. The Egyptian tortoise can produce one to five eggs, but the normal clutch size is two to three eggs. The marginated tortoise can produce up to nine eggs in a clutch. The actual numbers produced can be quite variable. Occasionally, multiple clutches can be produced in a year. When this occurs, there is usually a duration of roughly 30 days between nestings.

Instead of collecting them, you may be able to allow the eggs to remain where they are deposited. Your location will determine whether you will be able to allow the eggs to incubate naturally in the ground. If your climate is as warm or warmer than the climate of the tortoise's natural range, it is possible that the eggs can develop in the nest. Natural incubation is usually not recommended because of the lack of control and the risks presented by the elements and nest predators—ants, raccoons, foxes, and others.

Female tortoises often will nest in the same spot or close to it year after year.

Problems With Egg Laying

If your tortoises are well acclimated, healthy, and normally active, the nesting process should not be a problem. Occasionally, you might have a tortoise that appears ready to lay eggs but cannot or will not lay the eggs. Most of the time, this tortoise will eventually either nest or evacuate the eggs without nesting, but as with everything else in biology, there are no certainties. If you notice a tortoise displaying nesting behavior, it is a good idea to note the day the nesting behavior began, along with the behavior's duration and the location of the nest. The weather conditions are also a good observation to note. These records of normal nestings can alert you if something is wrong or not normal, giving a base to compare the current behavior to. This is important for helping you determine when you should intervene if the tortoise does not nest as scheduled.

Once nesting behavior begins, tortoises generally lay their eggs in a day or two. If a week passes and there is still nesting behavior but no egg laying, then the tortoise should be watched closely. If the behavior goes beyond a week without any noticeable distress in the tortoise, continue monitoring the tortoise. Make sure you are watching closely, so you can intervene quickly. At the first indication the tortoise is in distress, get her to a veterinarian as soon as possible. Signs of distress include refusal of food, difficulty walking, or any other abnormal behavior or appearance. You must act fast because if the tortoise is showing signs of distress, her life could be in danger. Eggs that cannot pass along the normal tract can cause the surrounding tissues to die and rot, possibly resulting in hemorrhaging.

With an x-ray, the vet can determine if the tortoise is carrying eggs, and if it is necessary to intervene. Many times, the tortoise can carry the eggs to the next season and evacuate them then. Should the veterinarian determine that the eggs need to come out, there are drugs, such as oxytocin, that have been successfully used to induce a tortoise to lay eggs. There are more drastic measures, such as surgery, that can be taken if all else fails, but it rarely comes to that. Most of the time, things will go smoothly.

Incubating Eggs

The next task is to incubate the eggs. The eggs need to be maintained at a specific temperature in order for the embryos to develop properly. The sex of the developing tortoise is determined by temperature. This means you can exercise some control over the sex of the hatchlings by manipulating the temperature during incubation. There will be more on this topic later in this section. For most purposes, a temperature of 86°F (30°C) is recommended for incubation the eggs of *Testudo* species.

Setting Up the Incubator

To maintain the eggs at a stable temperature, you will need an incubator. A simple incubator consists of an insulated box, a heat source, and a means of controlling that heat source, such as a

The Incredible Egg

The tortoise egg is hard shelled with a thin inner skin that surrounds the contents and eventually the developing tortoise. The shell is made up of microscopic plates that allow the transfer of air and moisture between the inside and outside of the egg. It is for this reason that the egg needs to be incubated in a relatively humid environment, or the egg contents will eventually dry out. Although a humid environment must be provided, caution must be taken not to let the incubation medium get too moist or the exchange of gas is hindered. There is also the added risk of the egg absorbing too much moisture and cracking. It is for this reason that it is always better to incubate the eggs on the dry side.

When eggs are laid they are a translucent white to light yellow in color. When they are exposed to the air, they tend to become whiter if they are fertile. This process of becoming white is known as "chalking" and is usually an indication the egg is fertile, but it is by no means a guarantee the eggs will hatch.

thermostat. That is the basic setup. Anything else that can be added is only for the sake of maintaining a stable environment. While these additions are not necessary, they do make the process easier.

You can buy commercial incubators from farm and feed stores or through reptile publications and websites. However, most keepers choose to build their own incubator. This can add to the fun and experience of tortoise keeping. For the box, you can use any container, such as a fish tank,

This is an Egyptian tortoise egg just prior to hatching. The discoloration is caused by the baby tortoise tearing its way out.

plastic box, or Styrofoam cooler, or you can construct your own enclosure. For the heat source, a standard bulb or a ceramic emitter in a ceramic fixture can be used. The last major consideration is the temperature control, which can be accomplished by using a wafer switch or an old fish tank heater with the heating element removed. There are other means of setting up the incubator, such as using a thermostat as the temperature control, but these suggestions are probably the most cost effective.

The eggs should be placed in a container with a substrate that will hold moisture. Many keepers use sand, vermiculite, or perlite, or sometimes a mixture of the items listed. Another substrate that has arrived on the market that has some good properties for this application is ground coconut shell. It retains the moisture the eggs need but can be kept drier so the eggs can breathe.

Get Ready to Incubate

It is recommended that you have the incubator set up for at least several days before you think you will need it. By doing this, you can make sure the incubator is holding the correct temperature without exposing the eggs to temperature fluctuations while you adjust the thermostat. Also, if your tortoise happens to lay eggs earlier than predicted, you will be ready.

It is always a good idea to have the incubator set up and ready to go long before the eggs arrive. If the eggs do show up unexpectedly, you can place them in a container with the incubation medium and then place that in an area that maintains a relatively stable temperature, such as a boiler room or on top of a hot water heater until you can get the incubator constructed.

Standard practice when setting up the incubation medium is to moisten the substrate in a ratio of one part water to two parts substrate by weight. Note the consistency of the substrate at this ratio, because as the substrate dries out you want to maintain the same consistency (or just a little drier). The eggs are then placed in the incubation medium buried roughly halfway. Space the eggs far enough apart so that if any of the eggs go bad, they will not affect the good eggs. The container should have some small holes to allow an exchange of air, but you don't want so many that the substrate dries out too quickly. The container should then be covered.

Check the eggs every week or so for any eggs that have gone bad and to check the moisture level of the substrate. If the eggs are fertile, they will begin to chalk after a day or two but will sometimes show signs of chalking a few hours after they have been laid.

Temperature and Sex Determination

In tortoises, there are no sex chromosomes as there are in mammals and birds. The incubation temperature determines the sex of the offspring. There has been a limited amount of study done on this topic. The information that has been attained so far has shown that there is a precise temperature at which an even number of males and females are produced. Below that temperature, the number favors one sex, and above that temperature and the ratio favors the other sex.

This sounds simple enough, but there is much that is not known. For example, in some species of reptiles there is a second, and even a third temperature at which the ratios change to favor one sex or the other. So, the assumption about tortoises that below a certain temperature you get all of one sex and above that temperature you get all of another may not be correct.

With the limited studies that have been done, it has been found in some groups of *Testudo* that at a temperature maintained at roughly 86°F (30°C), you should get a one-to-one ratio of male to female in the hatchlings. Above that temperature, a higher number of females are produced, and below that temperature more males are produced. You should keep in mind that in biology, there is only one certainty and that is there are no certainties. Many keepers allow the incubator to vary plus or minus 2 degrees to increase the chances of a good mix of males and females.

Temperature also has an effect on the rate at which the egg develops, as is the case with all the other biological functions that occur in ectotherms. With a decrease in temperature, there is a corresponding decrease in developmental rate, and the embryonic tortoise takes longer to develop. With an increase in temperature, there is also an increase in the rate at which the tortoise develops. If the temperature is allowed to go too high, there is a corresponding increase in physical deformities that can be something as minor as multiple scutes to as drastic as missing limbs or even added limbs. From this, the importance of controlling the temperature should be clear.

Hatching and Hatchlings

At a temperature of 86°F (30°C), most of the eggs deposited by any *Testudo* species will hatch in 60 to 90 days, if the eggs are fertile and the embryo is viable. After 50 days, the incubator should be checked on a daily basis. If you miss a day or two, it is not critical. A hatchling tortoise can survive for well over a month without food after hatching, as long as it is in an environment where dehydration

After pipping, tortoises, like this albino Egyptian tortoise, will remain in the egg until the yolk sac is absorbed.

Yolk Attached

Occasionally, a hatchling tortoise will emerge from the egg before it has a chance to fully absorb the yolk. If the yolk sac is ruptured, it can lead to an infection fairly quickly. To remedy this situation, place the tortoise in a clean, small container with moist paper towel on the bottom. For the container, you can use a coffee cup or a small deli container. What type of container you use is not really important, as long as the tortoise's movements are restricted, so it does not rupture the yolk sac. Unless the tortoise is severely premature, the yolk will be totally absorbed in a few days.

is kept to a minimum. This will be the case if the incubation medium is kept properly moist.

Prior to the egg hatching, there is usually a noticeable discoloration of the egg. This is due to the tortoise scratching and tearing the inner membrane that surrounds it inside the egg. The discoloration usually occurs where the head is positioned and is accomplished by the egg tooth or foreclaws tearing at the membrane. The egg tooth is a small horny projection on the upper jaw just below the nostrils. Its only use is to aid the tortoise in punching a small hole in the egg, or "pipping" as it is often called. After the tortoise pips the egg, it will normally remain in the egg until all the yolk is absorbed into the body.

The time in which it takes eggs to hatch is extremely variable. Sometimes the eggs hatch quickly, and sometimes they take longer. It also varies from individual to individual, as some female tortoises lay eggs that hatch out in a short amount of time and some lay eggs that take longer to hatch. The point here is to be patient. If the tortoise in the egg is a healthy animal, it will eventually hatch. On the other hand, if the tortoise is weak and feeble it probably would not survive. It is usually not a good idea to help a tortoise hatch out, because the risk of harming a

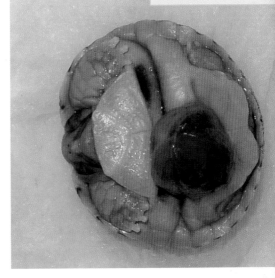

Sometimes tortoises leave the egg before they absorb the yolk, as this Egyptian tortoise did.

viable tortoise is greater than the chance of saving a weak tortoise. Allow the eggs to go full term and do not be tempted to open the egg early. If you notice the discoloration that was mentioned earlier, then it is probably all right to carefully open the egg—but do not remove the tortoise. Otherwise, it is best to leave the egg alone until you are certain it has gone bad.

When the tortoise first hatches, it is going to look deformed from being folded up in the egg. For the first week, the shell remains fairly plastic and will fill out to its normal shape if the humidity is maintained at a high level. The humidity will allow the tortoise to easily flatten out and attain its normal shape.

Baby tortoises are folded in half inside the egg, and it takes up to a week for them to unfold and assume the normal shape.

Oddities and Morphs

Every so often nature throws a curve into the development process, and an animal hatches or is born that would not otherwise survive in the wild. In some pet markets, many of these genetic or physical abnormalities are actually desirable. In other markets, these freaks of nature are looked down upon to the point that it is recommended that they be destroyed to maintain a genetic purity of the species. The animals in question are sometimes albinos or other unnatural color varieties (called "morphs" by most hobbyists), such as those missing black or yellow pigment. Other animals that would not normally be expected to survive in the wild such as multiple-limbed, two-headed, or other physically deformed tortoises are also seen as unique animals and desirable pets by some. As the breeding of these animals becomes more common, these types of tortoises have made their way into the hobby of keeping tortoises.

The albino tortoise is relatively common. Occasionally, a two-headed tortoise is able to survive, but that is unusual. Many other variations of color and form exist and are viable. What you have to keep in mind is that these animals are pets. There is no intention to release them back into the wild, so unless the animal is suffering or there is no chance for survival, there is no reason to destroy it. There is always going to be someone who will find a place in his or her heart for that animal.

Monetary Rewards

One final point that needs to be mentioned in this section because it does concern breeding tortoises is money. You really should not look at raising and breeding tortoises as a financial investment. There are many people who use investment as a selling pitch for some tortoises. If you consider the time it takes to properly raise your tortoise and the length of time it takes for your tortoise to reach maturity (normally upwards of ten years), you will quickly realize that raising tortoises for financial gain is a poor investment.

Two-headed tortoises are rare and do not usually survive, but the ones that live make perfectly fine pets.

Some keepers amass a collection that can and does make them money, but the time and energy they put into the project could easily make them more money in other pursuits. Those that do make a living out of raising tortoises usually have demonstrated their passion and commitment for the raising of their tortoises and only reap the dividends after a long time and an excessive amount of work. This, of course, does not consider one other very large and important factor—luck. Regardless of how much knowledge you have of a tortoise and its requirements, if you do not have one single pair that is compatible, then this stage in the life of your tortoise is sure to fail. This one last factor is ultimately the result of luck. This whole idea is being pointed out because many keepers seem to loose sight of the reason they keep tortoises. It is a rewarding feeling to raise a creature from birth to adulthood and watch the cycle continue. That should be enough to content any tortoise keeper.

Chapter 6

Health Care

The two most important points in the health of your tortoise have been constantly stressed throughout this guide, and they are going to be stressed here again. Heat and hydration are going to be your greatest insurance against ill health. This, of course, assumes that you have a healthy tortoise to begin with, and you are feeding it a good, varied diet. These factors will lay the foundation for a tortoise that should, in all likelihood, outlive you.

ealize that there are outside influences on your tortoise's health that you will not be able to control completely, if at all. Something as apparently minor as a short cold snap or a bird bathing in your tortoise's water bowl can have devastating consequences on your tortoise's health. Because there are a number of health-affecting factors you cannot control, it is critically important you control all the ones you can—diet, temperature, humidity, lighting, and other husbandry components. This chapter discusses the most common health problems seen in *Testudo*, how to prevent those problems, and suggestions for treating them.

If your tortoise becomes ill or injured, the chances for a successful recovery will be greatest if you consult a reptile veterinarian and the sooner you do, the better. Attempting diagnosis yourself is unwise, as there are many illness that present similar symptoms. When you adopt or purchase any animal, you are obligated to provide that animal with proper care, including medical care.

Hygiene

By purchasing a captive-bred tortoise, you will likely avoid many potential health problems, such as parasites.

Washing your hands before and after handling your tortoise is not only a good practice for the health of your tortoise, it is also beneficial to your own health. Reptiles in general have been implicated in the transmission of some diseases, so the practice of washing your hands with a good antibacterial soap and warm water is a good one. The habit of hand washing should be followed even if you have more than one tortoise in different enclosures and you are working from one enclosure to the next. If all your tortoises are

Finding a Reptile Vet

It is not always easy to find vets who are experienced with reptiles and amphibians. Here are some suggestions to help you locate a vet who can help with your pet tortoise. It is best if you locate one before you actually have an emergency.

- Call veterinarians listed as "exotic" or "reptile" vets in the phonebook. Ask them questions to be sure they are familiar with tortoises and *Testudo*.
- Ask at your local pet stores, animal shelters, and zoos to see if there is someone they can recommend.
- Herpetological societies—especially turtle and tortoise societies—are likely to know which local vets treat reptiles and amphibians.
- Contact the Association of Reptilian and Amphibian Veterinarians. Their website is www.arav.org.

kept in only one enclosure, the hand washing is not necessary for working within the enclosure but should still be done before and after working with the tortoises.

Parasites

One of the most common health issues of tortoises is parasitic infection. One type are ectoparasites, which are the parasites that are on the external surface of the body. These can take the form of ticks, mites, or maggots. The other type of parasites endoparasites, which are those parasites that live inside of the body. These usually take the form of worms and protozoa.

If you selected a captive-born and raised tortoise, you probably assumed it was free of parasites. While that is normally true, the ease with which a tortoise can become infected with parasites is amazing. Remember the bird in the tortoise's water dish? There is a possibility that bird has parasites that it can transmit to your tortoise. Any tortoise that is kept outdoors is at risk for picking up parasites. Indoor tortoises pick up parasites much more rarely, but it can happen, especially if you add a new animal to your collection.

Most healthy tortoises can live with a limited parasite load if they are fit and healthy. If the health should decline for any reason, the parasites can reproduce out of control. For the most part, the parasite does not "want" to kill the host, but if the host becomes debilitated for any reason, the parasite population will grow rapidly. Parasites have evolved to survive and reproduce as long as

A veterinarian familiar with tortoises is a valuable resource for the keeper.

the host does. There are checks and balances in place, such as the host's immune system, that keep parasite populations low, as long as the host is healthy.

The balance can be lost if the tortoise gets sick (other than by having parasites) or the parasites are not kept in check, partially by a good diet in the case of intestinal parasites. This is one of the reasons that fiber is an important component in the tortoise's diet. It is suspected that the fiber has a cleansing effect on the digestive system of the tortoise. With the ectoparasites, the situation is the same in that the tortoise can coexist with the parasite as long as the tortoise is healthy and the parasites are kept in check by being knocked off as the tortoise burrows, forages, and soaks.

An important thing to remember is that tortoises and their parasites evolved in the wild. As the parasites reproduce, the eggs and young leave the tortoise (through the feces or by dropping off the skin), and the tortoise moves away from the young parasites. In captivity, the situation is very different. The parasites reproduce as normal. However, the tortoise cannot easily get away from the next generation of parasites. They share the same cage. So, the tortoise keeps getting re-infested with each succeeding generation of parasites. This is an oversimplification and is not true for all parasites, but it illustrates how a parasite population can explode in pet tortoises.

The parasite load is usually high in wild-caught tortoises. While this can be overcome, it requires a great cost in time and money. Remember that as long as there is a balance between the health of the tortoise and the parasite load, there should be no difficulties for the two to exist together. The problem with this idea and the wild-caught tortoise is that the stress of collection is almost always overwhelming. Add to this the stress of being kept in overcrowded and often filthy and inadequate conditions before it ever makes it to the pet shop, and the balance tilts in favor of the parasites. The more time passes before the tortoise can be placed in suitable conditions decreases the chance that the tortoise will ever recover and survive.

If you do find yourself in the situation of being tempted to purchase a wild-caught tortoise, always ask how long the tortoise has been in captivity or how long the tortoise spent in overcrowded conditions. The shorter the time, the better are the chances of survival for the tortoise. This is one of the main reasons a captive-born and raised tortoise should be selected whenever possible.

Ectoparasites

Ectoparasites are a minor problem in tortoises, for the most part. Captive-born and raised tortoises rarely have ectoparasite problems. They can be quite common in wild-caught animals.

The two most common ectoparasites are mites and ticks. Mites are arachnids (like ticks and spiders) that are smaller than a pinhead. They are rarely found on tortoises. When present, mites can be found in the folds of the skin, such as those on the neck and legs. These are usually active and can be seen moving about if they are present. You can also find evidence of them from their dusty, grey feces and from their drowned bodies in the water bowl. Mites feed on the blood of their hosts and reproduce rapidly. If your tortoise has mites, you should act quickly to eradicate them.

Ticks are much larger in size, being up to 1/2 inch (1.3 cm) in diameter but are more often 1/8 to 1/4 inch (0.3 to 0.6 cm) in diameter and are not as active as mites. They are more common on tortoises than mites but seem to prefer the same locations. Like mites, ticks feed on blood. They do not reproduce quickly but are known to spread disease.

No Ivermectin!

Ivermectin is widely used as an insecticide, and veterinarians often prescribe it for ridding reptiles of mites and ticks. However, it can be deadly to use in tortoises, causing the animals serious neurological problems. Do not use it. If your veterinarian prescribes it for your tortoise, kindly inform him that you would rather use another course of action to be on the safe side. If vet insists, find another vet.

Wild-caught Mediterranean tortoises often carry ticks. Eliminate them as soon as you find them.

Eliminating Mites and Ticks If you encounter either of these parasites, they can be physically removed. Use a brush, like a small paintbrush, to brush away mites. For ticks, remove them carefully using tweezers. The tick can be removed by grasping the tick and, with steady force, pulling the tick backward and parallel to the skin. Make every effort to remove the head that is under the skin. If the head should break off, it should be left in and that site on the animal should be cleansed with an antiseptic.

It is also important that the tortoise's enclosure be thoroughly cleaned. If you have an outdoor enclosure, this is not realistically possible, and you should continue to monitor the tortoise for any reoccurrence and remove any more parasites that should appear. It will take time, but the parasites will eventually be eradicated.

The use of insecticides is not recommended. Some vets recommend the use of ivermectin as an external antiparisitic. It is diluted and sprayed on the infested animal. An injected form is used extensively in reptiles but affects tortoises adversely. *Do not use ivermectin with tortoises.* It is highly toxic to tortoises and other turtles, causing severe neurological damage.

Maggots One other ectoparasite that shows up occasionally is maggots. These are the larval stage of flies. They only become a problem if a fly is allowed to deposit eggs in an open wound. Tortoises have some deep, covered pockets that allow some parts of the body to be hidden by the shell. If a maggot problem is going to develop, it will be in these areas.

It is a good idea to give your tortoise an external once-over every time you pick it up. Pay particular attention to the places where the skin attaches to the shell and especially to the areas in the rear of the shell around the legs and the tail. On occasion, you should carefully push the tail up and out of the way so you can inspect the area beneath it. It should be emphasized that these parasites are normally not a major concern, because they are rarely, if ever, present on clean healthy animals. If you end up with a maggot infestation, take your tortoise to the vet as soon as possible.

Endoparasites

Endoparasites are the most likely parasites you will encounter in your tortoise. If the tortoise is an indoor tortoise and it comes from good, captive-bred stock, it is unlikely to have parasites. Anytime you add a tortoise to the group, there is a risk of introducing parasites or disease (this is one of the reasons to quarantine). The risk increases if you are mixing different species. This practice is not recommended, but if you are dealing with tortoises that have similar care needs, it can be done. The mixing of different species of wild-caught tortoises carries an extremely high risk to the health of all the tortoises in the group. Each tortoise might be carrying different pathogens for which the others have no immunity. This can cause serious problems and, again, is not recommended.

Tortoises that are kept outdoors will eventually pick up internal parasites; this is almost a certainty. The sources of transmission are virtually impossible to control because tortoises can pick up endoparasites from the ground, water, air, insects, and wild animals. This should not be a problem if you maintain the tortoises in good health.

Signs There are several signs to look for that will indicate to that your tortoise has been infected with endoparasites. The most obvious indication that something is wrong is if the tortoise has changed its behavior but all environmental conditions have remained unchanged. This means you will have to know what your tortoise acts like normally. You should be concerned if your tortoise should

Not All Mites Suck Blood

Sometimes you might find some tiny mites in the enclosure substrate that are smaller than a pinhead and are white in color. They are normally present only in organic substrates that are kept excessively moist. These areas can be found around the water bowl or in the area of the humid hide box. These particular mites are an aesthetic nuisance, but they pose no real threat to the tortoise. Cleaning the wet area and either replacing the substrate or keeping it dry usually eliminates the little critters.

suddenly stop eating (but remember that a tortoise may do this if the weather turns cool). This alone can cause the tortoise's health to move into a downward spiral and tip the balance in favor of any parasites that might be present. If the conditions gets worse, you may see other indications, such as closed eyes or a runny nose—signs of general ill health and not necessarily an indication of a parasitic infections.

Another indication of parasites is the appearance of the tortoise's feces. They should be firm and formed in the shape of a pellet. If the feces are runny without any shape to them, there is a good chance there are parasites present. This of course also depends on what you have been feeding your tortoise. High-moisture foods, such as melons and overripe fruits, will also cause runny stools. Sometimes, you may even see worms or worm eggs in the feces.

Nearly all wild-caught Mediterranean tortoises will have worms or other internal parasites.

If the parasites are not detected and eliminated, all of these signs will increase in severity as time goes on. If the tortoise begins to dehydrate because it is not taking water–which they sometimes do when they are not healthy for any reason–the eyes will start to have a sunken appearance. The discharge from the nose will sometimes increase with time, possibly indicating a secondary infection. There will also be a noticeable loss of weight, due to the tortoise not eating All these signs will get progressively worse over time, so it is very important to know your tortoise and try to catch any of these signs early. As soon as you notice a change in behavior, watch the tortoise carefully and make certain that it is warm and well hydrated.

If your tortoise shows any of these signs, the next course of action is to seek veterinary care. Be sure to take a fresh fecal sample to the vet with the tortoise. This will allow the vet to look at the sample under a microscope to determine if parasites are present. If you cannot get to the vet that day, you can refrigerate the sample or keep the sample in a cool place for a few days. Do not freeze the sample. Freezing will make a good diagnosis more difficult.

Types of Endoparasites There are two major groups of internal parasites that are commonly encountered in tortoises. These are the protozoans, which are single-celled organisms, and the helminths, which are parasitic worms.

The protozoans are a large group of single-celled organisms that are more complex than bacteria. In this group, those that are the most commonly seen in tortoises are the flagellates and amoebas. These are the parasites that are most easily transmitted and are the ones you are most likely to encounter. The tortoise can naturally live with a small number of these parasites present. If the tortoise should be stressed for any reason, these parasites can bloom and then become a health problem for the tortoise.

If these are detected early enough, they can be eradicated or reduced in numbers with the proper drugs. The most commonly used drug in the elimination of flagellates and amoebas is metronidozole. This is a safe and effective medication if used properly. Tortoises seem to have a high tolerance for metronidozole, so even the smallest tortoise can be safely medicated. The dosage is highly variable and is based on the application in which it is used. Follow the instructions of your veterinarian.

Necropsy

The autopsy of an animal is called necropsy. As unpleasant as it may be to think about, should your tortoise die unexpectedly, it is a good idea to have a vet perform a necropsy. This is especially important if you own other tortoises, as the procedure can detect an illness that could affect your other pets. A necropsy can also reveal some unknown flaw in your husbandry. It is important to refrigerate, but not freeze, the body to prevent decomposition. The sooner you do this after death, the more information the vet is likely to find.

The helminths include the flatworms, tapeworms, and roundworms. Those that are most commonly encountered in tortoises are the roundworms, although the others show up on occasion. The diagnosis for the helminths is similar to that of the protozoa. A fecal sample from the tortoise is examined under a microscope. The veterinarian looks for the eggs or the organism itself, which does not appear often. Occasionally, the tortoise will pass a worm in its stool, which can be quite large in relation to the size of the tortoise.

For the helminths, the drug of choice is usually fenbendazole but it depends on what species of helminth is found. The dosage will also vary depending on what course of action a particular veterinarian chooses to use. Fenbendazole is another safe drug, but there has been some recent evidence that some animals react adversely to the drug if it is used over a long period of time. This has not yet been documented in tortoises.

Seek A Vet

While access to antibiotics is relatively easy to come by, it is not recommended that you diagnose and treat your tortoise on your own. It is highly suspected that the overuse of the once very effective broad-spectrum antibiotic enrofloxicin, has led to the emergence of bacteria resistant to this particular antibiotic. Additionally, without doing a culture it can be difficult to determine which antibiotic will be effective against the pathogens. With this in mind, it is always the best course of action to seek out the advice of a veterinarian.

While there are other endoparasites, such as blood parasites, these are rarely encountered in the captive-born and bred tortoise. They can be common in wild-caught tortoises. Not a great deal is known about these parasites in tortoises because they are difficult and expensive to properly diagnose. Also, until recently, there has not been a significant interest in the diseases of reptiles and amphibians. Historically, parasites are usually found on necropsy, which is the detailed examination of a dead animal. For this reason, it is not known if these parasites are actually pathogenic or not.

In sum, parasites are frequently seen in tortoises, but as stated earlier, they are not always a problem. If they do go unchecked, they can become difficult to treat and possibly life threatening for the tortoise—plus expensive and disheartening for the keeper. Any problem with both internal and external parasites can be greatly reduced or even eliminated with good husbandry practices and by starting with a captive-bred tortoise.

Infectious Disease

Bacterial and viral infections are health issues commonly seen in tortoises, but little is actually known about how they affect tortoises. Bacteria are implicated in colds, pneumonia, and infections that occur after injuries. Bacterial infections are mainly the result of some kind of deficiency in the care of your tortoise, which causes the tortoise stress that compromises its immune system. This is not always the result of an intentional fault, but—with close attention being paid to the little details of husbandry—the occurrences can again be minimized or eliminated.

There are some common bacteria that are easily identified in cultures and as a result are easily diagnosed and treated. However, most veterinarians will choose to use a broad-spectrum antibiotic rather than to actually culture out the bacteria, because so little is actually known about the effects many bacteria have on tortoises in general. Additionally, many owners do not seem willing to pay for cultures, which is a shame.

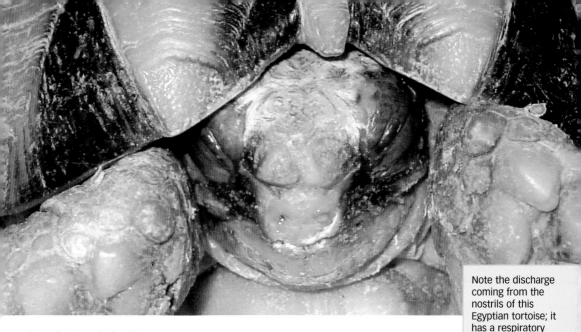

Note the discharge coming from the nostrils of this Egyptian tortoise; it has a respiratory infection.

Respiratory Infections

One common health issue that is usually caused by bacteria is respiratory infection. This usually occurs when the tortoise is stressed and the environmental conditions are suboptimal for that species.

The Russian tortoise is especially susceptible to respiratory disease. While the Russian tortoise can tolerate very cold temperatures, it cannot tolerate cold and damp conditions. In these conditions, the Russian tortoise will quickly develop a respiratory illness. If not treated quickly, the disease will progress rapidly. Thick, mucoid discharge from the nostrils is one of the first signs. As the disease progresses, it eventually moves into the lungs, causing pneumonia and respiratory distress.

It is hard to notice labored breathing in a tortoise because of the shell. If you take notice of normal breathing when the tortoise is healthy, you can see a difference in the pumping action of the head and legs when the tortoise is in respiratory distress. If there is congestion in the lungs, it can be heard with the aid of a stethoscope placed on the top of the shell. The lungs lay to the left and right of the centerline just under the top one-third of the tortoise's shell. The upper surface of the lung is separated from the lower surface of the carapace by a thin membrane.

If respiratory illness is suspected, make sure the temperature of the tortoise is at least 80°F (26.7°C) and be certain to soak the tortoise daily. Think of the normal advice for sick humans: keep warm, get plenty of rest, and drink plenty of fluids. This also works with tortoises. This line of thought even goes one step further to the similarities of cold treatment in humans. Veterinarians are now administering citric acid, which is reported to boost the immune system to help fight the infection; citric acid is a major component in orange juice. Keeping the tortoise warm and hydrated will help prevent your tortoise's condition from worsening and give you the time you need to get your tortoise to a veterinarian.

Herpes Virus

Viral infections are not very common in tortoises and almost nonexistent in captive-born and raised animals. There is one particular virus that is occasionally found in tortoises, especially in *Testudo*. The virus is a herpes virus, and it is extremely contagious when it is active. There is no cure for this virus, but there are antiviral drugs, such as acyclovir, that show evidence of suppressing the virus. During an outbreak, the virus can spread through a group of tortoises quickly, and those animals that contract the virus have a low chance of survival. Many of the aspects of the disease remain a mystery, even though this virus has been studied extensively in recent years. It is now believed that the virus is commonly present in tortoises, and it is stress that causes it to become active and life threatening. With the proper precautions, such as quarantining and good hygienic practices, the risk of your pet contracting a herpes virus is quite minimal.

The cheese-like matter in the mouth of this Greek tortoise is the result of a herpes virus infection.

Infected Wounds and Abscesses

Open wounds are another source of bacterial infection in tortoises. A tortoise can receive an open wound as a result of aggressive breeding behavior, an accident, or an attack by another animal, such as a dog, cat, or bird. In the event that your tortoise receives an open wound, you should, of course, get it to a vet as soon as possible. For the most minor cuts, place the cut under running water. Do not wipe the cut. Cleanse it with povidone iodine. Finally, cover the cut with a good triple antibiotic ointment. Try and

Reptile Fevers

When humans and many other mammals get sick, they often become feverish. The fever seems to cause the immune system to operate more efficiently. It also may make the body less hospitable to pathogens.

Since reptiles can't raise their body temperatures, it would seem impossible for them to get a fever. However, they can use behavior to mimic the conditions of a fever. When a reptile is sick, it will often seek out the warmest possible temperatures. Studies have shown that reptiles suffering from bacterial infections attempt to keep their body temperatures higher than normal. Additionally, reptiles that can't raise their body temperatures when they are ill are less likely to survive. What all this means for the keeper is that when your tortoise is sick, raising the enclosure temperature a few degrees—can have a positive effect and may improve its chances of recovery.

keep the tortoise in a clean, warm, and dry environment until the cut scabs over. A container with a towel or newspaper substrate is recommended for this.

Septicemia

Bacteria is implicated in septic infections that occur in tortoises, seen most often in tortoises that are under one year old. A septic infection is an infection of the blood and can be extremely difficult to treat. It is usually associated with renal failure, which in turn can lead to liver failure. The telltale sign of a septic infection is the presence of blood between the keratin layer and the bone of the shell. By the time a tortoise shows any signs of septicemia, there are usually the other signs

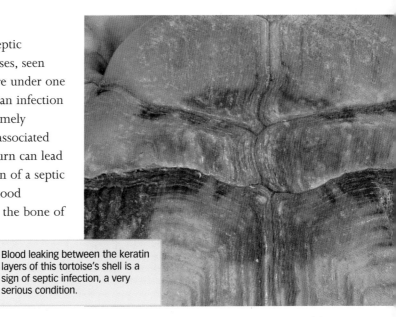

Blood leaking between the keratin layers of this tortoise's shell is a sign of septic infection, a very serious condition.

of illness that were previously mentioned, such as runny nose, sunken eyes, and lethargy. The tortoise should have seen a vet long before the infection progressed to septicemia.

Septicemia is mentioned here because if you ever do see these signs in a tortoise that you might be interested in purchasing, it is highly recommended that you pass on the animal because if you don't, the odds are high that it will pass on you. Septic infections have a dismal of a rate of successful treatment.

Metabolic Bone Disease

By far, the most common nutritional problem encountered among tortoises in general is metabolic bone disease (MBD). This is less commonly seen now than in the previous years of keeping tortoises, but it does show up more often than it should. This condition can be caused by a deficiency of calcium, a deficiency of vitamin D, or lack of exposure to ultraviolet light.

Calcium-Rich Plants

Almost every plant contains calcium, but some have more than others. Additionally, some contain forms of calcium that are more or less digestible than others. Here is a short list of plants that have high levels of calcium in a digestible form. It is not exhaustive, but these plants are fairly common in gardens and grocery stores.

- Cactus pads *(Opuntia)*
- Collard greens
- Dandelions
- Mulberry leaves
- Mustard greens
- Turnip tops

The unique trait of the tortoise is its shell, which is nothing more a modified rib cage. Because of the mass of the shell, there is a high percentage of bone in the total body mass. It is mainly for this reason that the calcium requirement of tortoises is so high. The first signs of calcium deficiency and MBD are softening of the shell and deformed jaws. If the problem is not corrected, the signs worsen and include deformities of the shell, impaired movement (from soft and easily fractured limbs), inability to eat due to severe jaw deformity, and muscular tremors.

Calcium Metabolism

A simple explanation of the controlling mechanism for calcium might give you a little insight as to the importance of calcium throughout the body and not just for the bone structure.

Because calcium is so important in many bodily processes, the balance of calcium in solution in the bloodstream is very important. That balance is maintained by the interaction of vitamin D, parathyroid hormone (PTH), and calcitonin.

When the precursor of vitamin D is digested, it travels to the skin. When the skin is exposed to UV light, the precursor is converted to another form of vitamin D. This form is transformed in the liver and kidney to yet another form of vitamin D. This final product is the form that is actually used in regulation of calcium levels.

Vitamin D, in conjunction with parathyroid hormone, increases the concentration of calcium in the blood. The parathyroid hormone increases the concentration of calcium by stimulating the release of calcium from the bone, retention of calcium by the kidney, and absorption of calcium by the small intestine. Calcitonin decreases the uptake of calcium when there are sufficient levels in the blood. As calcium levels increase, the parathyroid gland decreases the output of the PTH, and as calcium levels drop the parathyroid gland increases PTH secretion.

PTH also stimulates the production of the active form of Vitamin D, which in turn stimulates the uptake of calcium by the intestine. This is where the importance of kidney function comes to light in calcium metabolism. If the kidney fails, calcium is not replenished and continues to be taken from the bone. From this oversimplification you can see the importance of calcium in normal bodily functions and you can also see the importance the kidney plays in the process.

The best way to prevent MBD is to feed your tortoises a varied diet rich in leafy greens, supply a calcium supplement, and give them access to sunlight.

Tortoises and Dogs Don't Mix

One of the most common causes for traumatic injury is the overzealous actions of the family pet and more specifically the family dog. Most domestic pets are hunters by instinct, and tortoises make enticing prey. If you have a dog or a cat—no matter how well you trust them—never leave a tortoise unattended with any of these animals. Also, make sure that the tortoise is secure in its enclosure with no possibility of the other family pet having access. All it takes is one accident, and the feeling of letting your pet down will never go away.

Prevention and Treatment

The best way to avoid MBD is to feed your tortoises a varied diet, provide supplemental calcium, and expose them to UVB. It is much easier to prevent MBD than to treat it. If you suspect your tortoise has MBD, take it to the vet as soon as possible. Also, review your husbandry in an attempt to determine where the cause of the MBD may lie. The vet will generally take x-rays and perform blood tests to see if your tortoise does have MBD. If it does, the vet may prescribe calcium-rich foods, give calcium injections, recommend adding more calcium to the diet, or take other measures, depending on the reasons for and severity of the MBD.

Grooming

Grooming usually does not come to mind when you are thinking of a tortoise, but you may need to trim your tortoise's nails or beak. Overgrowth of nails and beak happens most often with tortoises that are maintained indoors on a nonabrasive surface. It can be controlled by providing a substrate that will provide some wear to the beak and nails. Some keepers provide an abrasive material by adding flat rocks as furniture and as a feeding surface on which the food is placed. Slate or flagstone is commonly used for this purpose. If you closely monitor the length of the beak and nails, you can avoid major operations by trimming these items on a regular basis instead of an as-needed basis. If you allow them to get too long, they become more difficult to trim.

Trimming is always easier if you get your tortoise used the handling and used to the necessary tools before you actually need to trim. You can condition your tortoise by first handling it on a regular basis to gain its trust. For both the nails and the beak, you can use an emery board or nail file for light sanding. Because the keratin is laid down in layers, it is always easier to sand or file in the direction that the nail is growing and parallel to the surface. This would apply to both the nails and the beak. Most tortoises will allow you to do this if done in a non-threatening manner, but it does take a little time to gain their trust.

Pyramiding

One of the more common developmental problems encountered by tortoise keepers is called pyramiding. This describes a condition in which the individual scutes of the carapace grow vertically rather than horizontally. Over time, the scutes take on the appearance of little pyramids. There is a great deal of controversy surrounding the cause of this. The common belief is that it is caused by feeding too much protein and overfeeding in general. However, this does not appear to be the case. Recent research strongly suggests pyramiding is the result of an interaction of diet and environmental conditions. Recent studies have shown what many long term keepers have suspected all along: Heat and hydration are the most important factors for obtaining a smooth, normally formed shell. Hatchlings in particular need adequate humidity for normal development and should be a higher relative humidity than the adults. This is another reason why heat and hydration are so important.

For more drastic beak trimming, a rotary file is recommended. If the growth of the beak does reach the length that would necessitate the use of a rotary file, you should have a veterinarian or another person who is experienced in this procedure to demonstrate it, so you can avoid any risk of injury to the tortoise. Many vets will choose not to do this procedure without anesthetizing the tortoise, if the overgrowth is too extensive. It is a good idea to practice a little preventive maintenance to avoid the expense and stress of anesthetizing.

For the nails, you can purchase dog or bird nail clippers at most pet stores. It is important to know how far back to clip the nail to avoid cutting the quick. Holding the foot of your tortoise up to the light you can usually see where the vein ends. You don't want to cut below that point. If you should cut into the vein and cause some bleeding, any styptic pencil or powder will stop the bleeding and reduce any chance of infection. You can apply a dab of antibiotic ointment to the nail, if you wish.

Hibernation Issues

Hibernation was previously discussed in the breeding chapter. Here we discuss some health problems that are related to hibernation. Some of these health problems are not only restricted to hibernation.

If the tortoise should experience freezing temperatures (and you notice this before the tortoise

Some rocky areas and some rough surfaces in the enclosure will help wear down your tortoise's nails.

succumbs), do not raise the temperature too quickly. Bringing the tortoise into room temperatures is sufficient until the tortoise comes around.

When you notice the tortoise moving somewhat normally, you can then slowly move the tortoise into more comfortable temperatures. If the tortoise should experience subfreezing temperatures, it is a good idea to get the tortoise to a vet to rule out any chance of frostbite.

For those tortoises that are hibernated indoors, they should be checked weekly for proper hydration or any sign of respiratory problems. Many keepers go so far as to weigh the tortoise to monitor weight loss, which is a good idea. Any weight loss over 5 percent of the original body weight should be cause for concern, and the tortoise should be brought out of hibernation and rehydrated. Afterwards, monitor its condition closely and be prepared to visit a vet.

Some tortoise keepers have experienced attacks by feral animals during hibernation. This is most commonly experienced by keepers who hibernate their tortoises in boxes that are stored in a basement or garage. The culprit is usually a rodent. The risk of rodent attack can be minimized by making sure the container in which the tortoise is stored is secure and placed in an area that will be difficult for rodents to access. Periodic inspection of the container will alert you to attempts by rodents to gnaw into it. Hard plastic containers are more difficult than wooden ones for a rodent

Because hatchling tortoises, like this baby Hermann's, grow so quickly, they are at a higher risk of MBD and pyramiding than adults.

to get through. If the tortoise is attacked, the injury usually occurs on the legs. If you do find such an injury, slowly bring the tortoise up to normal temperature, treat the wound with a triple antibiotic cream, cover the wound with gauze, and get it to the vet as soon as possible.

Conclusion

This section has covered most of the more common health issues that you are likely to encounter in the care of your tortoise. Knowing your tortoise's normal behavior and habits will help ensure that if something does go wrong, you will notice it early. As it has been stressed all along, if you should suspect something is wrong, be sure the tortoise is kept warm and well hydrated until you can get the tortoise to a veterinarian. Your best resource for finding a vet is to contact other tortoise keepers in your area through your local turtle and tortoise club or pet shop. Not only can other tortoise keepers help you find a vet, but most are willing to talk tortoise and share their experience, which is always helpful.

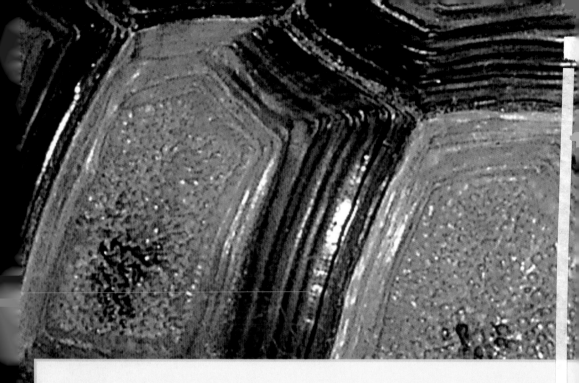

Hopefully, this guide has provided many of the answers to the questions that have come up in your quest to provide the best care for your tortoise. Of course, not every situation that you may encounter has been covered here, but this book does in fact offer a good foundation to make the keeping of your tortoise an easier task. In the pages following this section, you'll find a list of references that were used in preparing this book in addition to other useful titles, too. Some of the titles that are included may not be readily available but can usually be ordered through any large library, or they may also be obtained through other tortoise enthusiasts. However, most of the listed references are not hard to locate at all and it's highly recommended that they be reviewed in order to gain a better understanding of the information presented here. Additionally, seeking out these references serves as a good vehicle for networking with other tortoise keepers, which is half the fun of keeping a tortoise anyway.

Conclusion

On a personal note, I hope you will find that tortoise keeping can become an extreme passion for you, as it has for me. What started out as simply keeping a pet tortoise during my early years has developed into a major part of my life, in addition to the lives of those around me. For this, I would like to express sincere appreciation to my wife of 24 years, Kathy, who had no idea of what she was buying into when she decided to marry me. I would also like to express a great big thanks to my two girls, Amanda and Danielle, who do not realize that the level to which their dad has taken his interest is not really normal and that not every family worries about taking in the tortoises during inclement weather. To my family, thank you for putting up with this odd passion, and to my friends, thank you for sharing that passion.

References

Arnold, Nicholas E., and Denys W. Ovenden. 2002. *Reptiles and Amphibians of Europe*. Princeton: Princeton University Press.

Barnard, Susan M., and Steve J. Upton. 1994. *A Veterinary Guide to the Parasites of Reptiles: Protozoa*. Melbourne: Krieger Publishing.

Barnard, Susan M., and Lance A. Durden.2000. *A Veterinary Guide to the Parasites of Reptiles: Arthropods*. Melbourne: Krieger Publishing.

Bowman, Dwight D. 2003. *Georgis' Parasitology for Veterinarians*. Philadelphia: W.B. Saunders Company.

Deeming, D.C. 2004. *Reptilian Incubation: Environment, Evolution and Behavior*. Nottingham: Nottingham University Press

Iverson, John B. 1992. *A Revised Checklist with Distribution Maps of the Turtles of the World*. Richmond: J.P. Iverson Publishing.

Lagua, Rosland T., and Virginia S. Claudio. 2004. *Nutrition and Diet Therapy Reference Dictionary*. Ames: Blackwell Publishing.

Mader, Douglas R. 1996. *Reptile Medicine and Surgery*. Philadelphia: W.B. Saunders Company.

McArthur, Stuart, Roger Wilkinson, and Jean Meyer. 2004. *Medicine and Surgery of Tortoises and Turtles*. Ames: Blackwell Publishing.

Pennak, Robert W. 1988. *Collegiate Dictionary of Zoology*. Florida: Krieger Publishing.

Kuzmin, Sergius L. 2002. *The Turtles of Russia and Other Ex-Soviet Republics*. Frankfurt: Chimaira.

Kohler, Gunther. 2005. *Incubation of Reptile Eggs*. Melbourne: Krieger Publishing.

Kutchling, G. 1999. *Reproductive Biology of the Chelonia*. Berlin: Springer-Verlag.

Peterson, L.A. 1977. *Edible Wild Plants*. Boston: Houghton Mifflin Co.

Schleich, Herman H., Werner Kastle and Klaus Kabisch. 1996. *Amphibians and Reptiles of North Africa*. Koenigstein: Koeltz Scientific Books.

Tabaka, Chris, DVM. and Darrell Sennehe. 2004. "Egyptinan Tortoise-*Testudo Kleinmanni*." www.chelonia.org/Articles/tkleinmannicare.htm

CLUBS & SOCIETIES

Amphibian, Reptile & Insect Association
Liz Price
23 Windmill Rd
Irthlingsborough
Wellingborough NN9 5RJ
England

American Society of Ichthyologists and Herpetologists
Maureen Donnelly, Secretary
Grice Marine Laboratory
Florida International University
Biological Sciences
11200 SW 8th St.
Miami, FL 33199
Telephone: (305) 348-1235
E-mail: asih@fiu.edu
www.asih.org

Society for the Study of Amphibians and Reptiles (SSAR)
Marion Preest, Secretary
The Claremont Colleges
925 N. Mills Ave.
Claremont, CA 91711
Telephone: 909-607-8014
E-mail: mpreest@jsd.claremont.edu
www.ssarherps.org

The Tortoise Trust
BM Tortoise
London
WC 1N 3XX
England
E-mail: tortoisetrust@aol.com
www.tortoisetrust..org

Turtle Survival Alliance
504 Ladin Lane
Lakeway TX 78734
Telephone: 512-608-9882
E-mail: Lisa@TurtleCenter.org
http://www.turtlesurvival.org/

VETERINARY RESOURCES

Association of Reptile and Amphibian Veterinarians
P.O. Box 605
Chester Heights, PA 19017
Phone: 610-358-9530
Fax: 610-892-4813
E-mail: ARAVETS@aol.com
www.arav.org

RESCUE AND ADOPTION SERVICES

American Tortoise Rescue (US)
23852 Pacific Coast Hwy #928
Malibu, CA 90265
www.tortoise.com

ASPCA
424 East 92nd Street
New York, NY 10128-6801
Phone: (212) 876-7700
E-mail: information@aspca.org
www.aspca.org

RSPCA (UK)
Wilberforce Way
Southwater
Horsham, West Sussex RH13 9RS
Telephone: 0870 3335 999
www.rspca.org.uk

Turtle Homes (worldwide)
PO Box 297
Merrick, NY 11566
http://www.turtlehomes.org/

WEB SITES

Russian Tortoise
http://www.russiantortoise.org/

California Turtle and Tortoise Club
http://www.tortoise.org/

Chelonian Research Foundation
http://www.chelonian.org/

World Chelonian Trust
http://www.chelonian.org/

MAGAZINES

Herp Digest
www.herpdigest.org

Reptiles
P.O. Box 6050
Mission Viejo, CA 92690
www.animalnetwork.com/reptiles

Photo Credits:

R. D. Bartlett: 18, 119
I. Francais: 3, 8, 62
Paul Freed: 10, 115
James Gerholdt: 1, 35
Jerry R. Loll: 87
S. McKeown: 17, 25, 30, 69, 71

J. Merli: 29, 80
Susan C. Miller: 36, 55
M.P. and C. Piednoir: 67, 82
Jonathan Plant: 100
K. H. Switak: 12, 19, 60, 65, 74, 118, and cover

All other photos by the author.

Note: Boldface numbers indicate illustrations.